ALZHEIMER'S
TRIPPIN'

with George

Diagnosis to Discovery in 10,000 Miles

SUSAN STRALEY

ISBN-13: 978-1-7335465-0-8

Edited by: Margaret Juhl and Mary McNeece

Printed in United States of America

Published on Amazon
Susan@susanstraley.com

Dedicated to:

Caregivers;

Kind-hearted souls that support them;

All those who housed us, fed us,
and reached out to us on our trip

Table of Contents

Why Go?

"When life isn't going right, go left"
Haylea S. on Dove candy wrapper

George and I had sometimes talked about what we would do if one of us was diagnosed with a severe mental illness or dementia. "I am outta here!" I would assert. No sense in ruining two lives because one of us got sick.

In fact, I told him before and after our wedding vows that it was just a formality and I was not really promising him I would be there if he got sick.

I have always been one who loves freedom and wants to wander. Even growing up in a lovely safe family, I was the child who would disappear. My parents and siblings and neighbors often were frantically searching. At three years old I was found three blocks away playing in a mud puddle.

As I teenager I didn't run away, but I dreamt of it often. As soon as I graduated from high school I moved to a small town in northern Wisconsin. There I worked, made friends and explored.

Maybe this deep urge for freedom and discovery is why I took to riding bicycles. George and I began going on weekend trips to ride different trails with friends. In 2008, the day after George semi-retired, we took off on a ride around Wisconsin. It was just George and me on an adventure that lasted 40 days. We hauled our tent-cots, computers and clothing in carts behind our trikes. I loved the simplicity -- ride, search for food and water, sleep, pack up and do it again.

Right after our ride we loaded up a moving truck and relocated to Florida. There we met other bicycle adventurers on the Withlacoochee State Trail. We loved our life sharing rides, meals and fun with others who had stories of their own hiking and biking adventures.

I was still working part-time for George's machine design business. George was still calling in to the office and making decisions. As I look back now I can see that one of the first big clear signs that he wasn't thinking right was in 2011. The business started to falter and he refused to return to Wisconsin to work on it. I was furious and frantic.

We had friends that were business smart and George respected them. They convinced him to turn the business over to me as President and Owner. I was surprised that he agreed. I wonder now if they saw that he was not competent

1

to do the job. They told us it would be good for the business to be woman owned.

I slowly transitioned into the position of authority. Sometimes I would see things that George didn't see such as design flaws or financial needs. I would wonder, "When did I get smarter than George?" He was always the smart one. Still I didn't recognize the symptoms.

It was in 2014 when we were in the process of selling the business that it became very clear that something wasn't right. At staff meetings George would say things way off topic. He would make sales calls to the same customer more than once a day. The staff in the shop came to ask me if George had Alzheimer's disease because he was asking the same questions over and over.

I was scared. I wanted to run away, but I had to stay and get the business sold. Our financial future depended on it.

I look back now and realize I should have recognized the symptoms so much earlier. Some signs were there. I hear that a lot from other caregivers. Once the diagnosis is made, they look back in time and say…"Oh so that change in personality (or habit or ability) was probably due to the loss of brain cells."

I remember getting mad at him a lot. I thought it was retirement that was changing him. It was actually the dementia making him less interested in his work.

Once the business was sold, we returned to Florida and I had to convince George to get tested. He thought it was my cognitive ability that was declining. So we both got tested. And then again because he passed the little test at the research center!

After lots of testing, scans and many months of doctor visits we finally got to a definitive written diagnosis in June of 2015, "Normal pressure hydrocephalus (water on the brain or pooling of spinal fluid) and probably Alzheimer's."

Oh my! I REALLY wanted to RUN AWAY!

My sister is very nurturing. When my mother had Alzheimer's I took care of the checkbook and she did the nurturing. She knew to clip the nails and inspect the feet and take her to the beauty parlor.

I didn't WANT to take care of George. I didn't want our fun life on the trail with friends to stop.

I had heard stories of those with the disease getting mean. Oh my! How my heart would break if George was mean and afraid of me.

Another big fear I faced was of being left financially destitute. My mother had died with Alzheimer's disease in 2013 and spent the last of her funds in a nursing home before having to rely on government Medicaid. I knew first-hand how financially devastating this disease can be.

If one spouse spends down the family finances, what happens to the surviving spouse? How do they finance their retirement years if all the money is gone? I talked to George about divorce for strictly financial reasons. He cried and asked me to please wait until we had celebrated our fortieth wedding anniversary. That was coming up in August.

A big source of pride for George was our long and loving relationship. I couldn't move forward until after our anniversary.

OK. So if I can't fix it, I had to get moving. Go! "Head for the hills!"

I started to plan a trip to celebrate our forty years of marriage. I thought of it as a kind of "last hurrah" for George and for "us." We would see family and friends, we would see some of the places we had wanted to see and we would attend a recumbent tricycle gathering on a beautiful trail in northern Idaho.

Now, part of me knew we couldn't afford to spend some of our precious nest egg with a long trip. Another part of me said our time together was short and we needed to make the most of it. Would I regret going? Would I regret not going?

I decided to go and try to keep expenses as low as possible while still enjoying ourselves.

This book is the journal I kept on this trip. I kept it on-line as a way to keep our family and friends informed about how we were doing and where we were.

I also kept it as a memory for us; I knew George's memory would fade and my memory is always muddy. Having experienced loss of loved-ones before in my life, I already knew that guilt is part of grief. I wanted to record the good experiences to counter act the grief that was to come.

The travel journal turned into something so much more. The journal became a way to document our effort and ability to still enjoy life and each other even as George lost more and more of who he was before.

What I didn't foresee was it became a place of support for others caring for loved ones with progressive dementia and an education for those that surrounded us as I exposed the reality of day-to-day life with dementia.

Don't let the number of pages in this book scare you. I promise you will glide through the days and experiences as we did. Plus... there are a lot of pictures.

May you experience moments of joy every day.

Day 0 – Driving with Dementia

May 22, 2016

Tomorrow we launch our awesomely amazing adventure in celebration of our fortieth wedding anniversary.

The goals:
- <u>Enjoy the journey</u>. Don't just push to the next destination, but enjoy the people, the sites, the experiences along the way;
- Have so much fun that we don't get homesick for our friends and neighbors back home;
- <u>Keep the costs down!</u> Three months is a long time on the road, and we aren't camping. We are staying with Evergreen Club members (a travel club) and with friends and family... A couple of Airbnb's, a KOA or two, an occasional discount motel. Picnics instead of restaurants as much as possible; and

- Ride new trails and re-experience old trails with our recumbent trikes.

I will be doing all the driving on this trip. George no longer drives. When he was diagnosed at The University of Florida Byrd Alzheimer's Institute in Tampa, FL, (which I highly recommend if you are within driving distance) Dr. Smith (Yes, that is her real name.) didn't just slap down the diagnosis, write a prescription, and send us on our way. I have heard that is what many doctors do. Instead, Dr. Smith sat down with each of us alone and then with us together. She explained how this diagnosis was going to change our lives.

One of the things she told us was that George should be tested for driving competency. Now that he had the diagnosis, if he got in an accident, even if it wasn't his fault, an insurance company could deny payment. Why? Because we knew he was driving with reduced cognitive ability. The competency test would prove to us and the insurance company that he is still a competent driver.

It took a while to find a place that does such tests. In the meantime every time George wanted to drive somewhere or offered to drive, I reminded him of what Dr. Smith said and that we had to wait for the test.

This kind of testing is not done through the DMV or driver's education places, it turned out. This kind of testing is done through a place that helps those in rehabilitation (after surgery or accident) to get driving again. The place I found was through the University of Florida driver rehabilitation program at UF Health in Gainesville, FL. The test cost us $400 and was not covered by insurance.

Fortunately for me and others, George failed the test.

There are several reasons why a person with dementia should not be driving.

- Reduced peripheral vision;
- Inability to look ahead of the car in front of them and anticipate actions; and
- Slower reaction time -- the thoughts have to find a pathway around the damaged parts of the brain and that takes time.

I am so grateful to Dr. Smith for helping us get over this hurdle in a respectful way.

Day 1 –Our First Travel Club Stay

It is our first day of our fortieth anniversary trip. I was wide awake and up at 4:30 a.m. George used to be the one to plan the packing of the van. He was good at it!

He has already lost the skill it takes to pack a car so that everything fits and we can still easily get to the packed lunch. Today, I told him which items to take to the car first and went out with him to help him find a good spot in the van to place each item.

Once on the road I had to turn us back around three times to get something or do something I forgot to do. Thinking for two people while traveling is new to me. Fortunately we never got further than a few blocks away from home before we remembered something else.

We are staying for the first time with members of the Evergreen Club. Evergreen Club is a membership organization of travelers that share their guest room with other travelers. The guest hands the host $20 to cover the costs of breakfast and cleaning the linens. We have been told it is a fun way to travel. I was nervous about it, but I joined to save costs so we could do this trip. Tonight is our very first guest experience.

We arrive in our destination town, Chipley, FL (near Tallahassee), by noon! I had told our hosts we would arrive around 4:00. There is a state park just south of town. We went there and ate our PB&J lunch.

We got EVERYTHING out of the car so we could get the trikes out. Then we put EVERYTHING back in the car and went for a ride.

We rode down to see the falls of Falling Waters State Park and then through the town of Chipley, FL.

When we got back to the car, we had to take everything out of the car to put the trikes into the car. I was rushing to do this because George (with his dementia) has the tendency to just pick up the trike and head for the car even though I remind him about having to remove the stuff first.

We sat at the back of the van to take off our bike shoes and put on our tennis shoes Then I was done and I popped up to get stuff taken off my trike and take more stuff out of the car. George says, "Where's my other thing?"

I didn't know what he was talking about. When I looked at him, one of my shoes was sitting next to him. But I had two shoes on, so what the???? I looked down; I had on one of my shoes and one of George's shoes. I laughed a lot on that one.

That's one of my goals on this journey is to go with the flow and laugh a lot... to enjoy the journey, whatever happens.

Our hosts, Glenda and Bob, have a guest book and a picture of each of their guests, and their hosts where they stayed when they traveled. Under each picture are the names, dates, and location. What a great idea!

They have been members of Evergreen Club since 2010. They made us feel comfortable and sat and chatted with us a long time.

George and I had our evening picnic on their patio with the cat....

Thanks to our Evergreen hosts for a good visit and a good accommodations! Tomorrow we head for New Orleans.

Day 2 –Losing Language in New Orleans

Bobby and Glenda had breakfast with us and it was great to have fun folks to chat with. I like this Evergreen experience! After breakfast Glenda packed up some of the leftover fruit salad for us to take with us, yummy with pecans, coconut, strawberries and apple.

We took pictures of each other, said our goodbyes and George and I headed out to the car.

The car was running! There was no key in the ignition! I had to stick the key/fob in the ignition to shut the dang thing off!

I am suspicious that George pushed a button on his key fob, while hauling stuff to the car earlier, but I don't know.

Either a Louisiana wayside or Mississippi wayside had some beautiful wood art created with the trees that were killed during Hurricane Katrina.

George took this picture while we were going through a long tunnel.

In New Orleans we stopped at a grocery store to buy our supper. Mary and Robert, our Evergreen hosts, live in a home built in the late 1800s. The place is in an older, poorer area right next to a bar. A gathering of men with beer bottles and cigarettes in their hands observed us parking our vehicle.

Mary and Robert have a home and a side lot on one of the old narrow streets about ten blocks from the levee in New Orleans. The lot adjacent is made into a beautiful garden, with a locked gate. When we were let in through the gate we entered a haven and sanctuary in the city.

Mary and Robert have traveled a lot and had many interesting things.

George and I dined on the porch with the pooch.

Mary explained that the gathering of men on the corner is a good thing. They are regulars and watch out for things. They know her and that she often has travelers. Mary provided a tarp and helped me cover up the trikes in the back of the van.

Our hosts went out and provided us a key to lock up if we go out. "Make sure the dog doesn't get out," they instructed.

After dinner we went for a walk. I unlocked the gate but kept it closed and told George not to open it until I distracted the dog. George stood by the gate. I found a toy and threw it and it worked, the dog pounced after it. I said, "Go go go!" George just stood there looking at me. I pushed George (rather vigorously) out the gate and closed the door behind us just before the dog arrived back at the gate. George looked at me puzzled and angry. It occurred to me that even though I had explained what I planned to do, he did not comprehend. He not only was losing his ability to speak clearly, George was losing his ability to understand language.

I hugged his arm and smiled at him and explained why I pushed him out the gate ahead of me. I was learning to show my love for him with my facial expressions and touch and not rely so much on words.

(For more information about how I deal with George's symptoms, be sure to read <u>Alzheimer's Trippin' With George – The Journey Continues)</u>

We started down the street and shortly after passing the group of drinking and smoking men on the corner, we were about to pass a dumpster and out from behind it comes a big man pulling up his zipper. I guess he was surprised to see us, "I am sorry, ma'am, I am so sorry about that."

Mary tells me that taxes are assessed by the width of the lot... or were in the early years anyway. Lots are often narrow and deep.

I don't know if you can tell how massive the tree is (pictured below), but you can see the two poles in front of them, yes? ... with the weird markings?

A closer look...

The white is actually the remains from thousands of flyers being stapled to the poles over the years.

After a long walk we were almost back "home" when we passed where the trolleys go to rest at night.

Tomorrow we stay at the same home, but during the day we ride a trail north of Lake Pontchartrain.

Day 3 – 5 – Orleans to Mississippi

I asked our hosts where we might go for education and viewing regarding the 2005 hurricane Katrina. She said go look at the ninth ward. It was the worst hit area.

In the ninth ward we saw an area with houses and streets still in need of repair. And we saw some new homes that were built to replace the old.

We thought we had seen most of it. Then we saw several blocks with newer stylish solar homes, each home is unique. Not at all the public cookie cutter homes that I expected.

Wiki says:

"On December 3, 2007, Make It Right Foundation, founded by the actor Brad Pitt, committed to rebuild 150 houses in the Lower Ninth Ward. The houses are sustainable, energy-efficient and safe. Make It Right homes were designed by award-winning architects from New Orleans and around the world... Said Pitt: "I walked into it blind, just thinking, 'People need homes; I know people who make great homes.'"

I drove us to Slidell and to the terminus to the Tammany Trace Bike Trail.

Right next to the trail, a pond full of blooming lily pads.

On the bike ride back to our car we stopped at a bridge where the water below had turtles that started swimming toward us. Someone is feeding the turtles!

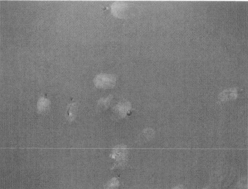

At a grocery store I bought salads for our dinner. George wanted ice cream. I helped him eat a pint in the car. Calories burned, Calories replaced... plus some.

Driving in Mississippi

M i s s i s s i p p i

I like that we learned how to spell that in grade school. It is coming in handy right now.

Our hosts helped us haul our luggage from the garden gate to the car.

If you like to drive to sightsee, then you need to add Hwy 10 and Hwy 55 on the south and west side of Lake Pontchartrain to your list of places to drive. We first were amazed that there was a major interchange with several layers of highway crisscrossing each other all over water. Wow! This thing must have cost MUCHO dinero!

Then this highway on cement pillars above water and wetland went on and on and on...

We were so amazed; isn't this why we travel? For these moments of awe and discovery?

I learned later it is 22 miles, one of the longest bridges in the world over water.

The Natchez Trace Parkway is a road with no road crossings and no stop signs. The speed limit is 50. It is supposed to be great for biking. There are signs along it reminding motorists to give bicyclists three feet, "It's the law."

We were getting within 30 miles of turning off the Natchez to head toward Amory where our next Evergreen lodging was located. Then the GPS went out. It said I needed a disc and the disc couldn't be found. I had no maps. I rely on the GPS and my iPad.

Fortunately I was able to use cellular on my iPad. I mapped out the route and then wrote it down turn by turn in case the iPad cellular disappeared. It did!

Our next travel club hosts were in northern Mississippi.

Nelson is 78 and still chops wood and cares for their home.

He plays guitar and Bess plays the dulcimer. They have a musical group that plays at nursing homes and local events.

They told us about their vacation cottage in Iuka. It is very near where we stayed in the Botel on our tricycle ride from northern Illinois to Inverness in 2014. I didn't remember that we stayed in Iuka until I looked back at our blog. See, it is good to get these memories written down!

George was beginning to show signs of dementia that I could not ignore before and during that ride in 2014. I had expressed concern to our friends and the children had observed changes in him. I did not write about it then.

Tanglefoot Rail Trail.

The Tanglefoot Trail is about 40 miles from Nelson and Bess' house. I am so grateful George can still ride beside me.

In New Houlka we noticed short little cement sheds.

They are storm shelters! We need some in the many mobile-home neighborhoods in Florida.

Back in Amory, it started to drizzle. That is perfect for catching up on this journal and staying out of the heat at the local library. George is still able to read and he watches movies on his iPad.

Tomorrow we drive a LOOONG way and end up at a KOA just east of St. Louis. There are many trails in Madison County, Illinois and some of them loop so it should be fun.

Days 6 – 8 - Bike Madison County, IL

Yesterday I forgot to mention something I learned from our host, Nelson. He was trying to read some small print and didn't want to put on his reading glasses. So he was peeking through a slit between two fingers. "It puts it into focus," he said. I tried it and it worked! If you are too vain to wear glasses, you can always do this...

We headed toward East St Louis, Illinois. Below is our picnic spot at a Missouri wayside. The part of Missouri we drove through was mostly flat flood plain turned to farm land.

Around 5:30 p.m. I drove into an industrial area. The GPS said we had reached our destination. I was doubtful until I saw a KOA sign. When we turned in we were amazed at how such an ugly neighborhood could be made quiet and nice with fence, bushes, trees and grass. We are staying in a KOA cabin.

It looked pretty clean before we moved all our stuff in.

Supper was chips and salsa and a can of soup and some carrots. Did I mention we eat vegetarian?

Madison County has several loops of bike trail. Tomorrow we ride a loop. We are here three nights.

George doesn't have any book to read. He finished one and the other doesn't hold his interest. Now he hovers next to me. He can no longer think of projects or activities on his own most the time. He depends on me to think and plan what to do. I am hoping we will come across a used book store or a free library box tomorrow.

I have an electric cooking unit that I used to make breakfast and dinner. I am learning to juggle while George sits, watches and waits.

Day 7 we ride the trails through a variety of landscapes.

We didn't get bored.

George and I squeaked our horns over and over as we rode though the underpasses, smiling and giggling.

We went to a McDonalds and shared one large coffee and three cookies. I was going to get two cookies but the clerk said, "Three for a dollar." Warm chocolate chip cookies and the coffee were very good -- $2.05.

I found a Goodwill store. We got several books for George. One I had read before and was pulled into the story, <u>Lovely Bones</u>. It did the trick. He is reading! Yeah!!!

At camp we take out his bike so he has a comfortable place to sit and read.

Later in the afternoon George was ready to go for a walk. I saw on the map we were near the Lewis and Clark Memorial Park.

There a volunteer told us some facts and stories.

How much meat did each man eat each day on average during the training and expedition?

Answer: Nine pounds of meat!

What kind of meat did they like best?

Answer: Dog meat!

We were at the Mississippi River and near the Lewis and Clark launch site.

On **Day 8** we biked to St. Louis. We stood on a bridge and watched a barge pass under us.

We crossed over an island to a bikes-only bridge that used to be part of Route 66. I pushed the button on the kiosk to listen to the song.

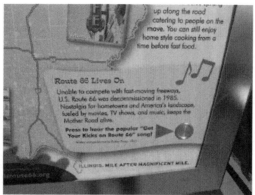

Then we began to dance. I love these shared moments of smiles.

The trail on the Missouri side of the river headed south and had a few hills.

Lots of fragrant flowers by the trail....

And heavy industry.

In some places the levee is just a cement wall. We weave in and out through large metal gates.

In my effort to find a place for us to picnic, I aimed for a park. We had to zig zag quite a bit and when we got closer the buildings looked like they had been bombed. Some of their roofs were caved in; some windows were missing. Yet it appeared people were living in them.

I made the executive decision to find a different picnic spot. George wanted to stop. I said, "I just don't feel comfortable staying here."

Back on the trail by the river we encountered art.

29

We found our way around road blocks to get to the Arch. I knew there was a park at the base of the Arch, and restrooms too.

The Arch is right there!!   Oh man! But we couldn't get there.   They had the whole area blocked off for construction.   A few blocks inland...

I found a restaurant with outside tables that was closed for the holiday so we got a table in the shade.

We are done with the big city; we head back across the Mississippi.

It became a hot afternoon. The ride back on the Illinois side had bumpy roads and several long miles on a rocky gravel path at the top of a levee. NOT FUN!

Tomorrow we drive to Rockford, IL to visit with our daughter Jodie and her husband Carl. Watch out kiddos, here we come!

■■

Just a simple request, before you set this book down and walk away, please leave a short review on Amazon. All it takes is one or two sentences to help others know if this book fits them. Thank you, Susan

Days 9 – 10 – Stutters and Lost History

Day 9, May 31, 2016, we were on the road heading North by 7:00 a.m.

At lunch, George had a hard time ordering; he stuttered. This is a symptom of his brain loss. I was told by the doctor that the normal pathway is gone. So the brain is firing and re-firing as it tries to find another pathway to get to the next part of the word or sentence.

We arrived at Jodie's and soon she took us to try to find George's sister and brother-in-law. Last George had heard from them (about six months ago) the brother-in-law said they were going into a nursing home. George's sister had dementia and her husband was in ill health and unable to care for her. Due to HIPPA (privacy laws) we were unable to find them. We were not given any information other than, "They are no longer here."

Later Jodie made veggie pizzas that were very yummy. George is happy! Look at that smile!

In the morning on **Day 10**, over morning coffee, Jodie showed a real interest in talking with George about his childhood and his past. He enjoyed spending time with her and sharing what he remembered. We feel so blessed to have her in our lives.

Later in the day we went to go visit my parents' graves. First a stop at the grocery store to pick up a flag for Dad's grave.

And on display are the chips that are made in Rockford, IL. MRS. FISHERS! We were raised on these chips. I think they are awesomely good.

I didn't resist. I bought a bag. Now my brother, who is reading this, is hoping they will last until we meet up with him in Colorado. To him I say, "Dream on!" And my sister who is reading this may hope they will make it five days until we reach her in northern Wisconsin. That may require greater will power than I possess.

A flag and some chips for Mom and Dad.

Back at Jodie's we pulled out the colored pencils and started coloring. Jodie and Jenna (our grandson's girlfriend) joined us and we sat around chatting and coloring like kids. Coloring is a new activity for George. It is something George can do while I am otherwise occupied (cooking, planning, mapping, blogging).

I found an adult coloring book made of note cards. I assign George to color the cards so I can give out thank you cards to all the nice people we meet on this trip.

Jodie announced that she and Carl were going to take us out to supper and afterward they were going to take us to the Bamboo restaurant where our grandson works as a cook. We would get dessert there.

I can feel my pants getting tighter just thinking about it.

Now off to get dessert in downtown Rockford. .

Thanks to Jodie and Carl for treating us to supper and desert! WOW! Tomorrow we will drive to visit with our Wisconsin biking friends.

Video Record Now

Right after George was diagnosed I pulled out the camera and tried to video tape him talking about his past. Already his ability to think of what to say or even remember things when asked was fading. It was a good idea, but already too late. The videos are too painful to watch. He doesn't say much, just his nervous, tearful giggle.

Getting to a firm diagnosis takes a long time.

ALZHEIMER'S TRIPPIN' with George

I have looked through our older videos and sadly they are of places and events which all seem insignificant now.

Over time his movement has changed and I wish I had video recorded him more. It would be so nice to see him laughing his hearty laugh, telling stories, dancing and running up some stairs.

My advice to you is record your loved ones now. Capture their voices, their movements and expressions, their stories now. Don't wait for a special occasion, a firm diagnosis or infirmity. We are all temporarily able. Do it now!

Day 11 – 14 - Friends of Gold

June 2, 2016, on our way to Madison, WI, we stopped in Durand and did laundry. We broke into the bag of Mrs. Fischer's Potato Chips and ate an apple!

We arrived at Kathi and Karl's home. They rent in an independent living complex. We feel comfortable with these folks who are down to earth and have been our friends since before 1990.

Karl was diagnosed with early stage dementia and the first thing I notice in their apartment is a large iPad-like wall display with the date and time.

Kathi came home from the grocery store with the ingredients for a new healthy vegetarian recipe. Kathi isn't vegetarian, so this was for us! Thank you, Kathi!

We walked the bike paths to the Fitchburg afternoon farmers' market. Then Kathi and I chopped vegetables.

Today I was able to talk with my son on the phone. It looks like we can join him for a BBQ this Saturday. I am excited to see them.

Day 12, George and I set out on a walk in search for breakfast. We got just a couple blocks before we decided to return and get our jackets. "Welcome to Wisconsin in June," I said.

I studied the iPad for how to get to Panera's. I tell you, my directional thing in my brain wasn't working and that scares me! We walked a mile one way and it just didn't feel right. I asked someone. She told us it was the opposite way.

Directional impairment was one of the first symptoms I noticed in George. I tell myself to pay attention for more clues that I might be losing cognitive function.

It was a pretty detour anyway.
Later we went for a trike ride of course.

We saw lots of "Little Free Library" stands. It is fun to see the different designs.

If you have been wondering what to do with all those old CD's, albums, and DVDs...

After 28 miles, we were back "home" by 1:30 p.m.

In the evening we walked over to the park by Kathi and Karl's home.

There is a children's water splash area with a farm theme in the park. I won't tell you what I said to George as I handed him the camera and climbed onto this rooster. I will tell you, he laughed his old hardy laugh. It is a joy to hear it.

41

Every Action Is a Struggle

Day 13 we went to visit friends on the way to our son's BBQ.

Our friend Elinor had a stroke months ago. She is a very healthy and strong woman, we were all shocked. She has made remarkable progress. As positive and strong as she is, she shared, "I am so tired of having to think hard to do anything."

Can you imagine suddenly having to struggle to do the simple things you used to do? To struggle to open a jar or a door, type an e-mail, set the table, walk and talk? She has come so far, but the constant struggle is exhausting. After she says this I realize that this exhausting struggle is similar to what a person with dementia experiences. This could be why many people with dementia sleep a lot.

When we arrived at my son's, we parked and walked toward their apartment. My granddaughter spotted me and came running. What a nice greeting! My heart is full.

While I was there, Abby and I got to play catch with a stress ball she had made with flour and four balloons. The game of catch was awesome! We kicked off our shoes and felt the grass on our feet -- smiles and laughter like old times.

Jeremy was cooking burgers and brats on the grill.

We drove back to Madison for another night at the home of Kathi and Karl.

Tag Them Now

Our new ID bracelets and other mail had arrived while we were staying at our friends' home.

43

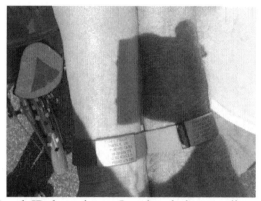

These are Road ID bracelets. I ordered them online. I have our names, our city and state and two emergency contact phone numbers.

George's says "Dementia, be nice to me."

There are six lines, so you could include medical information.

Getting lost can be an early symptom of dementia. Even if you don't expect your loved one to wander, an infection, dehydration, exhaustion can contribute to a sudden reduction in cognitive function.

I have been told by experts to tag your person and yourself early on. I always wear mine; if I get knocked on the head, I want someone to be contacted that knows George needs care, too.

Karl and George both were diagnosed with dementia "probably Alzheimer's." Alzheimer's disease currently cannot be definitively diagnosed until after death with an autopsy. This morning they were both looking happy and doing well. We compared ID bracelets.

Unfortunately one of the symptoms of Alzheimer's is also to take stuff off or refuse to wear something like this. George and Karl never protest; it is something we bicyclists wear in case we get in an accident.

I looked into GPS tags. I am sure they will get better and more affordable over time. Right now, a better item in our area of Florida is a sniff kit. They are available for free in Citrus County, Florida. They have trained bloodhounds to find lost persons using the scent kit. They are available through Find-M' Friends. Find-M' Friends is training dogs and sending them to police forces in other states that request one.

Day 14 and George is about half-way through <u>Lovely Bones</u>.

The target for our ride today was the Henry Vilas Zoo in Madison.

We came across a Farmer's Market where I stopped and bought two dozen eggs – one dozen for us to take with us and one to give to our hosts, Karl and Kathi.

"Nice hat!" I said.

He said, "Come back next week, it's always changing."

I put the eggs in the trunk of my trike and hoped we had a smooth ride home.

The Vilas Zoo is free to enter. As we entered the Herpetarium I wondered what a Herpetarium is....

The first display we came to was all these HUGE hissing cockroaches...

Yes... they are ALIVE!

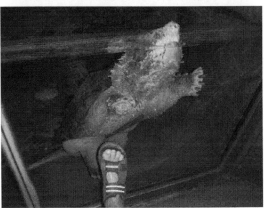

We biked 20 miles.

Find Your Tribe

I am learning that it is important for caregivers to seek out emotional and practical support.

On our last evening with Kathi and Karl, Kathi and I sat out on the porch and it was wonderful. It was just she and I sharing stories. We talked about how we are learning and our lives are changing as we adjust to our husbands living with dementia.

Kathi shared with me some pointers that have worked for her,

carry a kit in the car with wet-wipes and an extra set of clothes;

don't argue; don't correct; be agreeable and interested instead, even if they are hallucinating.

It is one thing to logically understand you are not alone; it is another to feel it in your heart, to connect with someone who has the same experiences.

Besides, you learn so much from others. Something as simple as keeping a "diaper bag" in the car, can help you feel competent and calm when an unexpected mess occurs.

Day 15 – 19 Rhinelander Awesome Sister

Today, at the last minute, I realized we were driving by Stevens Point where our friends Rolf and Barbara live. George and Rolf had bonded over things mechanical and running a small business. I contacted Rolf, and they were available to meet with us!

They own the bicycle shop in Stevens Point that specializes in recumbent bikes.

Barbara and Rolf told us that they recently switched to using electric-assist trikes. This sounds like a great way to keep pedaling beyond injury and disability. This may be in George's future.

My sister and her husband, Dave, live in Rhinelander, Wisconsin, surrounded by the "Northwoods."

In the yard are a few pieces of art that Dave has created. Dave was diagnosed in 2015 with dementia. Mary and Dave are not as public about the news as we have been. Dave still carries on good conversations. He still drives and works part-time.

Their back yard overlooks the Pelican River.

Mary knows how to add the artistic touches to give a space some beauty.

I feel blessed to have Mary as a sister. Mary has arranged for some others to visit while we are with her, so we can meet up with more of our extended family. My ex-sister-in-law Sue and her husband Cal arrived shortly after we did. They are staying at a motel in town. All six of us went out to eat in downtown Rhinelander.

While we were at the restaurant, George started shivering. He had refused his jacket, and still when I asked he says "I'm OK."

I go and get his jacket anyway, and he is grateful.

At Mary's we don't feel obligated to just sit and visit. Our family feels comfortable reading books and magazines when we are together. Mary and Sue play several games of cards, and sometimes I join in.

I couldn't hook up to the internet because neither Dave nor Mary remembered their login for the Wi-Fi. Tomorrow I will try connecting at the library.

Mary covered a few outdoor plants. There are frost warnings!

Company, Computer, Coordination

Day 16 of our trip I was able to sneak out in the morning for a walk while George slept. It was cold enough to wear gloves, two sweatshirts and a scarf.

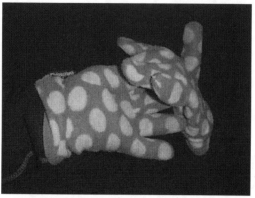

Later, George and I went with Mary to her yoga class in the basement of a church. We had packed our yoga mats for just such an opportunity. George never did yoga before his dementia symptoms showed up. I think he does it to be with me. I am his safe place.

We felt great afterwards. I went to the library to connect to the internet there. I couldn't. The librarian and I concluded it was my computer.

Back at Mary's my aunt had arrived. We sat around the table after lunch and talked for over two hours!

Then Mary and Sue played a few games of Spite and Malice. They giggle a lot when they play. Dave went out to mow the lawn. When I went out, he asked if I wanted to mow some. Yes! I like mowing.

George and I have some exercises we do. Last year George was having difficulty walking (an early symptom of the dementia). By doing the exercises assigned by the massage therapist, he has better balance and coordination.

Unfortunately, he doesn't do the exercises on his own. I have to initiate and do the exercises with him every time. He is supposed to do the exercises three times a day. If George were of his full mind, he would have the discipline to do the exercises religiously. I am not so regimented, and we often skip sessions and sometimes days. Even so, they have helped keep him mobile.

One of the exercises is doing the grapevine only the feet are placed right next to each other.

We do them until George is stepping on his toes a lot.
Then I took my computer to the computer doctor.

On **Day 17** I was up again before George to enjoy the stillness. It was a cool morning, and there was a mist lying over the river and dew on the grass.

When I returned to the house, George was up, dressed and soaking up some sunshine.

Cal and Sue called to meet us for breakfast.
In the restaurant, this sign had us wondering....

We were far enough away I had to get closer to read the small print.

After breakfast we stopped by the computer place so I could pick up my computer.

$58

I was pleased.

Mary, George and I hiked a trail that went around a lake. It had some steep ups and downs.

We warmed up as we walked, but we didn't dare take our sweatshirts off. There were lots of mosquitos.

George didn't stumble at all. When we got back to the car, George and I celebrated with a cheer and hug.

Back home I tried to connect up my computer.

I was so happy when I got up and running and my computer connected to the internet.

Day 17, after a couple days without writing in this blog, I struggle to remember what we did, what we saw, and the order of events. It is a good thing I am keeping a journal or the memories would all be lost.

Mary was cat sitting, and we rode over with her to feed the cat.

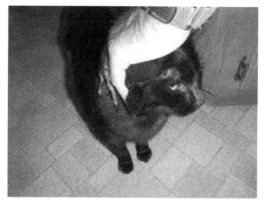

It was only 12 miles but enough to get our lungs and legs moving.

Dave asked if we'd like to do a fire for our last night at their place. "Sure!" I said.

We could view of the river from our fire circle.

Day 20 – 21 Blessed With Folks

Now back to Waukesha for my granddaughter's birthday.

We had time on the way to stop and see the machine design and manufacturing business we sold in 2014. George started this business and ran it for over 35 years. The new owners are finding new customers and taking care of the old customers.

Just 15 minutes from Rentapen was our next stop. Our friends Sandy and John had invited us for lunch at their home. Sandy is an amazing organic gardener.

We dined in the shade of a tree.

We are staying overnight with our Waukesha friends, Jane and Mark.

Every Friday night during the summer in downtown Waukesha, they block off the streets and have music.

What a great time!

Day 21 is my granddaughter's birthday!

In the morning Jane said they have a tradition of having pancakes on Saturday morning. "Do you want pancakes?" she asks.

"Sure!" George and I say in unison.

George yawns a lot these days. I think it is a symptom of the brain loss.

George was close to crying a lot today and is losing his ability to communicate. He cannot tell me what is bothering him. It may be just emotions without an explanation or reason.

One of the things with the brain is that it not only holds our memory, it holds our coordination, our emotions and our ability to solve puzzles. I fear the day when the emotions that come to the surface are anger and paranoia.

We go to my son's for my granddaughter's birthday. My daughter-in-law Mel is a loving Mom to Abby. Here she is posing with Abby's Aunt Tina.

Tina is mom to the munchkin.

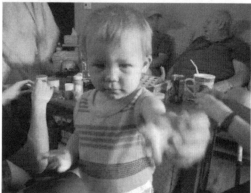

Tina makes good spaghetti and meatballs.

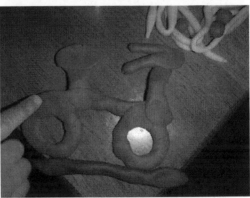

Back at Mark and Jane's, Mark had a few moments with me and asked about George. He said he noticed that he is moving around better than he was when they last saw us. It's the exercises that are helping him with walking and balance and getting in and out of chairs. But we don't have anything to stop the progression of the brain loss. Mark said he noticed that George sits looking at his iPad by himself more than before... less interaction.

I said it was good to hear that Mark noticed things. On good days I wonder if I am just imagining George's behavioral changes.

I was telling a friend that this journey is multi-layered. I am struggling with how brutally honest to be on this blog. This man, who was a genius in engineering and programing now can't figure out sometimes how to pack his suitcase or get logged into a new internet connection. How do I respect him while telling the story of this thing that is eating away at his brain cells, day-by-day?

I discussed this with my sister, and she said that our story will help a lot of people facing a dementia diagnosis. This journal can be a brutally honest look at the challenges and emotions along the way.

I am going to try to be honest and open about our experiences... the incontinence, the bathing, the getting lost and the strange conversations... all of it. Well... almost all of it....

Day 22 – 23 False Memories in Minneapolis

June 12, 2016 we were up, dressed and hauling stuff out to the car before anyone else was out of bed. I was writing a goodbye note when Jane stepped out and gave us each a nice hug.

We arrived at our travel club host's home before 2:00. We are close to a park and not far from some of the many bike trails in Minneapolis area.

Our bed for the night comes with a 14-year-old cat.

By 4:00 p.m. we were unloading our bikes from the car. I loaded up our dirty clothes on the trikes in case we came across a laundromat.

The Midtown Greenway runs East and West just a few blocks from our lodgings. But when we arrived, we were above and the trail was below.

I looked down the trail both ways and spotted a ramp two blocks away. Yeah!

Going down the ramp...

The Midtown Greenway was AWESOME! It is a highway for bikes and pedestrians. It was busy on a Sunday.

We passed under lots of bridges and crossed very few streets. When we did come to a street, the cars stopped for us. We found the Minneapolis drivers to be bike aware and respectful. Nice!

Whole low-traffic streets were designated bicycle boulevards.

On our way back we passed a car with artificial turf.

We ate our PB&J on our hosts' back porch. Geri joined us after a while. She doesn't like her picture taken, but she approved of this one.

I am torn between letting our hosts know ahead of time that George has dementia or not. Maybe they won't be able to tell, I think. But tonight it was obvious. As Geri and I chatted George would say things way off topic. Often his stutter and rapid talk made it difficult for her to understand, and I had to translate.

Tonight was the first time I heard George tell false stories. His memory and facts are getting twisted in his head. I didn't correct him. Instead I said, "Wow, I didn't know that!"

Turn off the Auto-Correction!

As a spouse and friend I am always ready to point out a false statement. I learned when caring for my mother with Alzheimer's disease that that is the worst thing I can do.

Someone with Alzheimer's or other dementia is losing part of their brain. Communication pathways are being obstructed. So it is reasonable that they will take bits of memory and fill in the missing parts. If you call them out on a falsehood or ask them to remember the way it REALLY was, you are hurting them and setting yourself up for conflict and frustration.

Let them live in their world; offer them empathy. If you and your loved-one are with other people and want the other people to know that the story is un-true. Say, "Isn't that interesting... I remember that differently."

Often you will hear those talking to someone with dementia asking them to remember. "Don't you remember?" or "Do you remember who this is?"

Instead help them save pride and belief in themselves by going along with their stories, introducing folks they may know, "Hey, look who's here, your friend, Sam!"

Make life easier for you and for them by not asking them to remember and not pointing out or correcting their false statements.

Day 23 was a great bike day! Minneapolis is a dream city for anyone that likes to bike.

I was biking along and George had fallen behind. I turned around and went back. His wheel had fallen off. A fellow biker stopped and helped find the parts that had fallen out of George's wheel hub.

We used my wheel as a model for putting the hub back together. In the process I discovered MY hub was loose!

Assembled again, the wheel now rolls. But... we have two extra parts!

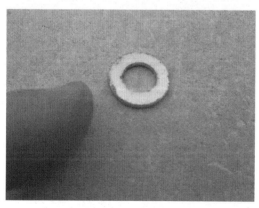

Tomorrow we plan to leave early to drive toward Idaho. We are heading to a trike rally there.

Day 24 - Across North Dakota

I had told Geri, our Evergreen Host in Minneapolis, we would be leaving early, and so she didn't need to make us breakfast. She created a little breakfast to go. Thank you, Geri!

We were in Fargo by lunch time. I pulled into a park to go for a walk and it started to sprinkle. We were not deterred. I pulled out my raincoat, and George used the umbrella.

Facing the long expanse of driving across North Dakota and Montana, I looked up book stores. BDS was close to downtown Fargo.

We walked in and WOW! There were piles and piles and shelves and shelves of books. I asked the owner if they had books on tape. He pointed us to a corner.

We got four or five books on CD to listen to. Total cost was about $60.

As we were checking out, the clerk asked where we came from, where we were going. He told us about Medora and Roosevelt National Park. He said if it has rained there, we should really stop because it is so beautiful with the wildflowers and the hills and rocks. He told us about the Medora Musical and glowed with enthusiasm.

George was doing well today and operated the CD player with ease...which was very nice. The first book we are listening to is a mystery with a bit of romance. It sure helps the miles fly by.

We stopped by a wayside later when the rain stopped and did our exercises. The wayside looked like an old gas station.

I picked up a brochure at the wayside on Medora, North Dakota. It said the musical plays every day at 7:30 MT. Mountain Time! We get an extra hour... we can make it there and go to the play!

As we were traveling my phone rang. I pulled off on a ramp and checked my messages. It was our property manager in Alabama saying that the people who had made an offer to purchase our rental property and then reduced their price on closing day were back with an offer at the original price.

Below is Medora, ND.

We drove up to the Music Welcome Center and got tickets. $33 each. Today was an expensive day.

$70 in gasoline
$18 breakfast
$60 for books on CD
$6 supper at Taco Johns (Taco Tuesday)
$3 coffee and M&Ms
$71 Musical Play tickets
$141 for motel room in Medora

We saw at the welcome center that the theater is outside with a backdrop of the hills. A guy was practicing being dead... I think.

I checked my email. There was an outpouring of advice, support and love from my friends and family regarding this blog and my honesty about George's dementia symptoms.

" George loves biking, meeting new people and seeing nature. You are making this possible. Enjoy the journey, the company and smile."
*****

"Your honesty is to be commended. The more we talk about and put dementia out to the public, hopefully, more research can be done.

... I did not realize until now that [my husband with dementia] cannot remember how to sign his name....something we all do so automatically. I wrote it out for him and he copied it...

75

Today I filled out paperwork for Financial Power of Attorney and had it notarized. I had him practice signing his name at home. It was either that or take him to court to get Conservatorship...jumping through legal hoops and have him take tests to prove his incapacity."
*****

"Think about how many people you may be helping. You speak for many people out there struggling daily. Opening your life to us who are not aware is helping everyone. Keep on writing..."
*****

I had an email from another property manager outlining the time line for closing on our Waukesha, WI property. I had no idea that the offer we countered was accepted! So now the last of our rental property will be sold (if they both reach closing). This will simplify our lives so I can concentrate more on caregiving and work and self-care. Good news!

After checking into our room we went back to the theater.

We took an escalator down to the seating.... outside!

I got on and then remembered that sometimes George has trouble with his balance and worried. I looked back and he was riding along just fine, getting on and off just as easy as I was. Smiles.

We edged past about six people already seated to reach our seats on the steep stadium seating I thought about it again. George would have stumbled so much last year. This encourages me to keep doing the exercises with him.

ALZHEIMER'S TRIPPIN' with George

This guy got on stage with his dog and I expected the dog would do all kinds of tricks. But the dog just sat there and the guy used him as a ventriloquist puppet. A real dog, but some kind of flap at his jaw that made it look like he was talking. It was so funny.

George was laughing a lot. We both had a great time doing something touristy.

Tomorrow we explore this area before getting back on the road.

I will need to spend some time in the morning hunting down some hosts. If we stayed in motels for this whole 90-day adventure, it would cost us $10,000. That is more that I want to spend for sure.

Tonight, though, is very nice to have a motel room to spread out in, stay up late watching late-night TV, and have a late night snack.

It has been A VERY GOOD DAY.

Day 25, Roosevelt National Park

There is a 37-mile loop through the Roosevelt National Park. The ranger at the visitor center circled all the shorter trails for us to walk.

There were several pull offs for scenic views. The first (and several) were for prairie dog towns. They are quite large (not the prairie dogs but the vastness of the "cities" they live in).

They are so cute I want to scratch them under the chin. The sound of the town added to the experience. There was occasional yipping near and far.

George pulled out his fancy camera. He still takes good pictures.

We were both so glad we didn't drive by this National Park. It is one of the most beautiful we have seen. Yesterday the guy at the book store said that if it rained, the wild flowers bloomed. We saw puddles, lots of green and flowers.

I saw a woman taking pictures of flowers like these orange ones below. I commented on how fortunate we were to be here after some rain. We got to talking. She and her husband are from Sarasota, FL. We are from Florida too! They are full time RV folks now. They sold everything. Then we learned she was originally from Milwaukee. We're from Wisconsin, too, near Milwaukee!

He was originally from northern Illinois.

"Us too!"

At this point I must have seemed suspicious because she quit talking and moved away. I guess I am a little over anxious to connect with people now that my partner is so quiet.

Early on I saw evidence of buffalo.

Then we came around a corner and there was a buffalo!

I thought that would be as close as we would get to a buffalo.

But then toward the end of our loop, we saw one lying right next to the road dusting himself.

George and I were smiling, "This is great!" he said.

Every corner we drove around was another fantastic view. George's camera captured some of the depth and breadth of it all. I don't know much about operating his camera. He knew which lens to use.

We realized you might miss the perspective of my foot in the picture. Smiles.

Our sightseeing was limited by the lack of facilities. Now 37 miles isn't far to travel in a car without facilities. But when you are stopping every mile to get out and walk or look, and you had three cups of coffee ... The last ten miles we didn't stop much.

We headed west on Interstate 94.

It was 7:30 before we finally stopped for supper and searched for a motel in Billings. All the Evergreen hosts (there are four) were not available to host.

Tomorrow night we hope to reach Missoula, Montana. We have planned two nights there with an Evergreen host.

Day 26 – 27 Missoula Frustrations

Driving again the scenery was awesome. The weather was quite windy.

I was able to work when we stopped to do laundry.
The wind was cold and strong.

In Missoula we went directly to a place to get some supper. Our Evergreen host told us about an organic grocery store with a buffet. Yum!

We went for a walk in the neighborhood.

We were still too early to arrive at our Evergreen host's home. We found a Dairy Queen in a Mall nearby. Then I got a quick haircut at Cost Cutters for $19.

At our hosts home we watched a movie with her; <u>Forks over Knives</u>. I was feeling very guilty for eating that Dairy Queen Blizzard.

I found **Day 27** to be tiring and frustrating. Usually, I roll with the punches and don't sweat the small stuff, but today was a roller coaster day.

Maybe it all started when my host turned on the news in the morning with the talk of the Orlando, Florida Pulse Nightclub mass shooting.

After breakfast with our host, George and I took our entire luggage out of the car to get the bikes out. Then we put the entire luggage back in the car. I said to George, "I am getting tired of this."

He said he was too.

We got on the streets and headed for the Bitter Root Trail.

We would find it. Then ride it a couple blocks and it would stop. Start stop, start stop. The sun seemed to be low in the sky; the cold air was brisk and dry. My eyes and nose ran constantly.

Each time we lost the trail I would have to pull out the iPad and study how to get back onto it again.

"Grrrr"

Finally we got on a long continuous strip heading out of town. It goes right along a noisy highway.

I just must have started out in a bad mood because after six miles we turned around. George agreed he didn't like the trail.

On the way back I got us off the trail and onto some side streets. I saw a sign for a museum. We followed the signs, and it went through what looked like a 1940's barracks or post war lodging.

We found the museum and paid our $6 to get in.

There were some things in the museum I remembered from my own childhood. OH MY! I am THAT old!

There were box cameras and instant print cameras and change makers.

The area is the place where a troop of solders (all black led by a white officer) tested using bikes for transporting troops. These guys climbed mountains, over snow, without the fancy gear that we have today to keep us warm and dry, and without the roads. Often they walked their bikes on railroad tracks.

The museum also had stuff on display outside.

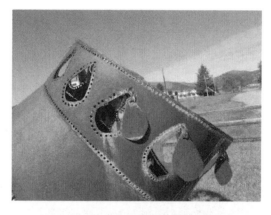

I set out to bike some trails in town.

We crossed a bridge and the trail ended. We turned around and took a different branch. That one dead ended.

Okay then, we will go through some neighborhoods. Missoula is surprisingly flat surrounded by mountains.

George noticed part of the hub on my wheel was missing! I have over 40,000 miles on my bike and never had any problems. I find it strange that both of our hubs are having problems. I can't help but think it has something to do with getting our bearings re-packed before we left home.

The quick release lever was missing too. We rode to a bike shop we had passed near the trail.

The bike shop was not for recumbent riders. They had no parts for trikes and they said that the hub was a CATRIKE proprietary part. Uh oh. I looked on my iPad and there is a Catrike dealer in Kellogg, ID.

I called them. Yes they could fix it. Then he said, "We probably don't have the parts. We will get it to work though."

We carefully rode my trike back to our car. I quickly called around to see if we could find a room close to the bike shop. In Wallace, Idaho one motel was booked. The next one I called had space. $119 with tax. I booked it and kicked myself for booking it.

Frustrated and worried. I had driven all this way to attend the Tons of Trikes Rally (or Tater ToT Rally) and now my trike was broken! I might have been OK with that but George probably won't ride without me. "Maybe I can assign someone to keep an eye out for him and get him back to our hotel," I thought.

We quickly packed and were back on the road. My plan was to go to Kellogg first and turn my bike in for repair before going back east to Wallace and our motel room.

When we got to Wallace I asked George what time it was. The bike shop closes at 5:30. He said it was 5:35. Dang! We went to the motel and I was kicking myself for booking the motel and then not getting to the bike shop in time to turn in my trike for repair.

We were hungry. "The restaurant doesn't open until 5," the woman at the front desk told us. "What time is it?" I asked. Five to five, she said.

Arg! We could have gone to the bike shop!

We went to get our luggage and put it in our room.

This is how unloading goes now. George gets his suitcase and stands next to me watching me as I gather stuff like phone, water, iPad, camera, computer and suitcase. I should be okay with this by now. I keep telling myself I will miss his presence someday. But today the self-talk was not working.

And $119 for a motel room, and they don't have an elevator. I told George, "I am going to drag my suitcase up the stairs. Thump thump thump."

The stairs were carpeted and there was no satisfying bang of protest.

Look at that picture! He loves me anyway!

After dinner I was exhausted. I wanted to go to bed. Instead we went for a walk with our jackets on. Next door is a hotel with a big sign "Suites $85." I kick myself some more.

We found the grocery store and bought something for our breakfast because... that is right folks. This $119 motel (with senior discount) DOES NOT INCLUDE ANY BREAKFAST.

Back in our room I worked on uploading pictures and checking email. I had an email from the realtor in Waukesha. The buyer's inspection was completed on the duplex, and the buyers want the moon and the stars from us. Yep, they want two new furnaces, re-doing the driveway, blah blah blah.

Then I opened an email from our Waukesha friends, Jane and Mark. We had left them the remainder of the Mrs. Fischer's potato chips. They took them with them to the Brewers Game and finished them off.

Smiles. Friends saved the day.

Did you leave a review yet on Amazon? All it takes is one or two sentences to help others know if this book fits them. Your opinion matters! Thank you, Susan

Day 28 – 32 TOT 2016, Kellogg, ID

Day 28 started out cool and rainy. As soon as the bike shop opened, we were there. The clerk was not so positive this morning that they could help us fix the hub of the wheel on my trike. They don't have the parts.

"But the web said you were Catrike dealers," I protested (whined, I admit).

"Yes," he said, "but we don't do a lot with them or have replacement parts."

The mechanic would be in later. We left the bikes and said we would check back in a couple hours.

We went to the motel where most of the trike rally was taking place.

There were just a few trike riders in the parking lot. I told them about my hub, and quickly one of them gave me a business card for a recumbent dealer forty-five minutes away near Spokane, Washington.

I called the dealer and he said, sure he could fix me up, he had the parts I needed. YEAH!!!!

We went back to Excelsior bike shop and took everything out of the van to put the bikes back in the van. We finished putting the luggage back in the van just as it started to rain.

We headed further west on Interstate 90.

Northwest Recumbents is in Post Falls, Idaho. A visit there is an experience. When I pulled in the drive the first thing I saw was a tandem trike with chickens around it.

The owner came and shook our hands warmly and welcomed us.

The owner had three other sets of customers besides George and me. He floated between tasks and customers with ease.

He asked if we were in a hurry and I said no. We were enjoying the space. We watched the goats and one of the customers took some popcorn from the popcorn machine on site to feed the goats. We fed the goats popcorn too.

I was looking at a hand crank trike. The neighbor helped me figure out how to get in, and George and I tested it out.

It is quite a workout for the core and arms. I could see us having one to ride on alternate days to improve our upper body strength and endurance.

When the owner, Gary Dagastine, got to working on our trikes it took maybe five minutes at the most. Done! Fixed! $30.

What a relief!

Back at Kellogg we stayed in the lobby and introduced ourselves to folks who looked like bikers.

There is a message board in the lobby. Monday is a ride to a restaurant in Wallace. Sunday evening is a potluck.

We met folks from California, Utah, Oregon, Washington, Texas, and Tennessee.

We unpacked our suitcases! Eight days without having to shuffle through a suitcase.... now we each have a drawer to shuffle through... YAY!!.

While emptying my suitcase I found a card from my sister! The sneaky woman had stuffed a card in my suitcase. I knew it was for my birthday which doesn't happen for a couple more weeks. But... of course I couldn't wait to open it.

What a wonderful surprise! I am so blessed!

When we returned to the lobby, Sylvia Halpern was there! She rode her trike solo from Oregon to Key West this past winter. She was a Warmshowers guest at our home in central Florida.

Look her up at "Travels by Trike." She is awesome. Each year she does a different tour during the winter and in the summer she stays in Portland, Oregon. Guess where we are going after Idaho! She says she is taking us on some of the better trails in that area.

We are official now. This is the tenth Tater Tot. It is our first.

We were fortunate to hook up with a group going to dinner. $29 with tip...

...including my giant margarita.

We socialized for a little bit longer in the lobby of the motel but by 7:30 we retired to our room for some quiet time.

Later I went down to the message board and posted what we planned to do tomorrow and I am keeping my fingers crossed that others will join us riding on the Coeur D'Alene Trail.

Day 29, we get to socialize with lots of fun people!

I had posted the day before about George and I riding from Cataldo to Harrison today, a 54-mile ride. I knew that 54 miles was beyond what many of these trike riders do. I had no idea if anyone was going to join us.

We got to the Cataldo and started to get ready to ride.

Two other couples arrived!

The Trail of the Coeur d'Alene's is among the most beautiful in the country. I did not encounter one ugly or boring mile on this trail.

We got about eight miles down the trail, and I could see we were approaching another parking access spot on the trail. There were about eight or ten trike riders waiting to join us there! I love when I invite folks and they show up!

The views were of wildflowers and grasses in the foreground, water (mountain stream, pond, river, or lake) in the middle ground. The scenery was always changing, always beautiful.

We encountered no moose today. We did see two deer, an eagle, pelicans, osprey, blue herons and lots of ducks.

When we arrived in Harrison we asked one of the faster riders, "Where to lunch?"

He said, "Up the hill."

We went up the hill and entered a restaurant there and sat out on the deck overlooking the lake. I watched, disappointed, as all the other trike riders arrive and not ascend the hill but go to the restaurant on the lake at the bottom of the hill. It took one hour from the time we ordered to the time we got our food! That is a long time when the person you are with doesn't talk anymore. George might make an observation of something he sees, but usually we just don't talk, unless I am thinking out loud.

We rode back to Harrison by ourselves which was fine. It was soooooo beautiful and the weather was perfect.

We arrived back at the hotel after the potluck had started.

At the motel I had a glass of wine (styrofoam cup) with Sylvia Halpern.

We watched an orange sunset. WOW!

In the opposite direction was a rising full moon.

It is clear that living well has not ended with the dementia diagnosis.

Day 30 started with George hovering while I was organizing stuff. I sent him down to the lobby for breakfast while I started the laundry. It was probably 20 minutes to 1/2 hour later when I got to the lobby.

He had opened the box I had sent down with him. In the box was leftover salad from the night before and about a 1b of sliced cheese.

George had eaten about 1/2 of the cheese and was still pulling off slices and eating them. I had to move it away from him.

Usually he makes himself oatmeal every morning. They don't have old fashioned oatmeal. I guess he must have just been unable to reroute himself onto some other plan.

I asked if he had breakfast and he said, "No."

"Do you want me to get your breakfast?" I asked.

"Yes," he said. When I got up to put something together in the lobby kitchen, he followed me. I put him to work making toast. I put a plate of eggs together for him and got some jam and a knife and fork.

A woman came in and said, "Wow" and something like "He is spoiled" and "Does his wife do this for him all the time?"

"She takes care of me," George said as he carried his plate into the lobby.

I felt the need to explain to her that it hasn't always been like that. "He has dementia," I explained.

I feel the need to tell folks... to explain his quiet, or when he says things in the middle of a conversation that has nothing to do with the conversation. And when I do sometimes explain it, I wonder if I should whisper it so he doesn't hear. I don't want to constantly remind him. It is always at the edge of my mind.

This morning when we got outside the group was already gathered.

After two or three miles we were by ourselves.

Entering into Wallace, George was ahead and had turned on the first street he came to. I called and sounded my squeaky toy/horn, he kept peddling. I blasted out a "GEORGE! NO!" and he did a U-turn and came back to riding behind me.

There is a railroad grade rise between Wallace and the east end of the trail in Mullen. It is about six miles of a gentle climb.

There were about a dozen riders hanging out in Mullen when we arrived. I love these friendly gatherings.

It was amazing to just float on down the hill almost all the way to Wallace.

One of the other bikers had told us the day before that the Mayor of Wallace said that it has been discovered that a Wallace Manhole Cover is the center of the universe. And there is no definitive proof that it is NOT the center of the Universe. So therefore, he declared, this spot in Wallace is the Center of the Universe until proven otherwise.

We went to the whore museum. $5 each for a little tour.

A standard position was $15 for eight minutes. They used egg timers. The maid would knock on the door if they went over time. The ladies could keep the tips.

The women averaged forty tricks a day, seven days a week. OH MY!

The sheriff got a cut to look the other way. Current residents still remember busy weekends when the line would go down the stairs, out the door, and down the block.

The place was in business until 1988. That is when the sheriff told the madam she better leave town for a while because the FBI was on their way. The madam and the girls left. They took very little with them. They were thinking they would be back in a couple days. But the FBI stayed for years... they were investigating the sheriff, not the whore house. They got the sheriff on profiting from drug trade, prostitution and more.

The madam and the ladies never returned and the madam sold the place in 1995. Everything is as it was when they up and left it in 1988. Except the food in the fridge was dumped, and there is a sign on the door of the fridge "do not open" since the odor is awful and still lingers.

We walked over to the mine tour.

The trolley takes us up to the silver mine.

When I took this picture, it hit me that George is leaning backward....

When we got back to the motel from our ride and tourist activities, it was already after 5:00 p.m. We needed to refill our waters and get ready for the night ride!

We rode six miles into the sun to the Snake Pit for dinner.

It turned out the guys we sat with had both lost their wives recently. They just found out about each other's loss at our table. Two months to the day for one, two months and ten days for the other. I don't know what to say.

The restaurant cat...

We were supposed to ride back in the dark. I was anxious to get going again. On the ride back I occasionally called out, "Here Moosey Moosey Moosey."

We rode slowly and as the dark descended, trikes with lovely lights began to pass us.

Day 31, I learned it is Taco Tuesday. But I didn't know that until too late.

By the time we got down to the motel lobby after I checked and responded to email, there were two table's full of trike riders drinking coffee and dining on the processed foods provided by the Fairfield Inn.

Some folks planned to ride a road loop that takes them to the top of a small mountain and then down and back to our motel. Some were getting a lift in a car to the top of the mountain and riding down.

I had already decided to use this day for paperwork.

While I was working, George read. But he kept getting up to watch what I was doing or walk around the room like he was looking for something to do... I asked him if he liked his book.

"Not that much," he said.

We had picked up a bunch of books from the Free Library in Rhinelander, WI. We walked down to the car passing through a lobby full of trike riders who are talking, a few reading, some checking their laptop computers and smart phones.

We picked up a couple mysteries out of the car and as we were going back through the lobby, I suggested he stay in the lobby in one of the lounge chairs. He looked happy about that idea. He stayed down there. I was a bit nervous about leaving him. I knew he didn't know his way back to the room. He couldn't use his phone to call me.

I handle the list of riders for our Withlacoochee Bicycle Riders. That morning I had received the public obituary of a fellow rider and friend. That was my signal that it was okay to put together a notice for our group. I was nervous about it and kept on typing up words and then deleting and starting again. I wanted to do it right for my friend that died and his wife. Writing it took longer than it should.

Finally I launched it and was relieved when later I got some good feedback from a few of our riders.

At 11:30 I got George from the lobby. He got up and said, "Nice talking with you," to the guy sitting on the couch next to him. I was pleased and surprised that he was able to carry on some conversation!

We went for a walk in search of lunch and then to the library to get paperwork scanned.

George pointed out that the Chinese Zodiac placemat had birth years that didn't go back far enough. His birth-year doesn't show up! Now THAT'S OLD!

The library doesn't have the ability to scan and send. They directed us to a printer around the corner. The printer charged $6 to scan and email the pages.

George and I did our exercises near the motel. I found out if we skip two days, he starts getting more wobbly on his feet. I feel guilty and berate myself. I really need to do this for him <u>every</u> day -- more more more.

We joined the late afternoon gathering outside the motel.

There was another potluck.

I noticed that Sylvia wasn't eating. I thought, well, maybe she is putting off starting so she doesn't eat as much.

Then she announced, "Taco Tuesday!" and she and a group walked off to visit Taco John's.

Day 32 was an awesome trail day.

Posted on the board in the lobby of the motel was a ride from Harrison to Plummer and back, with lunch in Harrison.

I decided to start the ride earlier further up the trail and meet them in Harrison. We packed a picnic lunch. George made the PB&J sandwiches without prompting from me!

George was ready to go so he picked up the lunch bag and stood watching me. I went and got some ice, got our water bottles and started to fill them. George put down the bag and came to help. Then he went and picked up the bag again.

I gathered our jackets and my purse, my iPad, the cameras and my phone. I brushed my teeth and put on sun guard. I sent out a couple last-minute emails. George stood quietly waiting, holding the bag. Finally we walked out to the car.

People haul their trikes in a variety of ways...

While driving I had so much stuff in the console next to us. My coffee was cold so I took it out and handed it to George and took my water and put it in the cup holder. George took the coffee cup and started to put it in the lunch bag. The coffee cup was open and had coffee in it. "Whoa," I said, "Don't do that. Wait."

He paused. I took my water out of the cup holder and had George put the coffee cup back in the holder. I then found a place to lay my water thermos.

We had put our trikes in the car the previous night after our night ride. The ride to the trailhead was maybe half an hour long on mostly country roads. It was a pleasant ride -- and... WE SAW A MOOSE!

George took these close ups with his camera.

We unload the van so we can unload the trikes.

I wrapped George's camera in a sweatshirt and put it in a bag so he could carry it with him on this ride.

We are ready to go at the Medimont Trailhead.
Oh oh... where are our bike shoes???

We had worn our bike shoes into our room after our night ride last night. I remember I had repeated to myself, "We WILL remember our bike shoes."

They were still in our motel room.

If we were going on a three mile ride I might risk riding without our clip-in shoes. On a recumbent trike if your foot sips off the pedal and hits the ground, it will hurt and you will probably break a leg. On a very short ride I can be careful, but keeping concentration up for 43 miles... naaaahhh.

We put the trikes and our stuff back in the van and drove back up the country roads to the motel. I think, "How can I turn this into lemonade?" And I think that we will drive to Harrison now and just start there with the group. But by the time we get to the motel we are fifteen minutes past the Harrison departure time. We just are not going to hook up with them.

Back to Medimont we went.

It is such a beautiful ride between Medimont and Harrison that we are soon glad we chose to start from that trail head.

At one point the beauty was everywhere and incredible. I was almost in tears.

There are others from TOT who pass us. We were not alone on the trail.

A bike bridge crosses the water and then does a 3% grade climb for 8 miles to Plummer.

The bridge deck is speckled with bird droppings, and the rise of the bridge is kind of stair-step design so we get brief rests from pushing hard. The rests are a chance to change gears.

At the top of the bridge other trikes and recumbents join us from both directions and a spontaneous social hour begins.

We finally break away with the idea of ascending the hill to Plummer a few miles so we can experience the ride back down.

At one point the biker in front of us has stopped, and a deer is on the trail in front of her. The deer watches us, then leaves the trail, then gets back on the trail and looks at us for a while. It then gets off the trail on the other side, turns around and gets back on the trail.

The biker clips back in and the noise scares the deer, but it only goes a few feet off the trail and watches us pass.

We went up the hill about two miles and back down and onto the bridge. Sylvia is there and tells us on her way down the hill she saw a bear and two cubs cross the trail in front of her!

When we were at this trail years ago, our friends also saw a bear in this same section of trail.

Sylvia offered to take our picture.

At the end of the day I check email. The realtors have sent paperwork to sign. One has reduced the price by $4,000 after the inspection. I have more paper work to do tomorrow.

Sleep Patterns Change

It is close to midnight when I climb into bed. George is still awake.

It used to be he would go to bed before me and be asleep when I got to bed. Then he would sleep a couple hours after I got up. Very early in the disease he needed more sleep and slept more.

In our early years we would go to bed at 9:00 and he would be up with the 5:00 a.m. alarm. He rarely had trouble getting to sleep.

Now, after the diagnosis of dementia, his sleep pattern is matching my own. This may be due to the un-ease he may be feeling due to the loss of brain function. He feels safe with me now and he needs to be near me often.

A symptom of dementia is that sleep patterns change. Those with dementia will sometimes sleep through the day and will be up much of the night. Sometimes unable to stay in the house, they will wander. This is difficult on any caregiver. I won't worry about that now.

Someone told me yesterday that True Value sells alarms to go on the door so if someone opens the door an alarm goes off. Good information to have for when this disease progresses.

I have also heard that melatonin can work to help your loved one sleep.

Days 33 – 35

Taking Over Prescriptions

June 23, 2016 I had real estate paperwork to do. We walked to the printer, stopping at the playground to do our exercises.

George, when he was first given the exercises, he looked at me angrily when I started to coach him through them. I said to him, "Look, you don't like me telling you what to do. I don't like this new role of having to tell you what to do. But with you having dementia, this is the way it is. So we might as well get used to it."

I am lucky that this message stuck. Now he goes along with it and smiles and that is a good thing for both of us.

After taking care of some work, George told me he was out of his medicine. He has glaucoma, and if he doesn't get his drops every night there is a big danger that he could lose some of his sight.

I had mixed feelings. I was frustrated that we would have to spend the afternoon getting his prescription filled. I was angry that he didn't tell me sooner so I could have planned when and where to pick up a refill, and at the same time I was glad he was able to tell me. I was grateful that he is still able to remember to put the drops in, and he can put the drops in himself. There will be a time; I am digging my heels in. I don't want to go there.

It is 36 miles to the Walgreens. While we were there, I bought a map of Oregon. The young girl at the checkout said she wouldn't know how to read a map.

I said, "Well you read it on google, don't you?"

She said, "No, I just push the button and my phone tells me where to turn."

Back at the motel I checked George's cosmetic bag and found a bottle of eye drops almost full.

That is my fault. I should have checked before driving to Walgreens. I put the new ones in the fridge. It's all good.

We went to sit outside and join the group gathered in the shade of a van in the parking lot.

Malott gave me a light beer. I usually don't drink beer because it tastes like ... beer. But this was pretty smooth and ... light. It went down easy, and the conversation flowed nicely.

We walked with Perry Butler to meet the group at the Mexican Restaurant. Perry owns the Casita trailer we saw in the motel parking lot and he lives in... Get this all you Lanesboro and Root River Trail fans... he lives in a condo in Lanesboro, Minnesota. Which condo? The big old school house converted to condos on the hill!

I gave Perry one of the books on tape that we had listened to for his long drive home.

George was chatting with Perry and turned to me and asked me what it was when we go someplace and hand them five bucks.

I was puzzled. "You mean Evergreen Club, where I hand them $20 and we spend the night?" George nods.

$30 for our salads and fries plus tip.

Wet Day

Day 34 turned out to be wet in more ways than one.

It was raining. I chose to hike the Pulaski trail near Wallace, ID.

I stopped at the Wallace Chamber to get directions to the trail. She said, "Drive to the mountain and turn left. Then drive to the mountain and get on King Street. Go one mile to the trailhead. It is well marked." Strange directions, but they got us there.

The signs on the Pulaski trail are incredible. They seem new, vivid, and well maintained. It is an 800-foot rise and two miles to the tunnel making it a four-mile round trip hike.

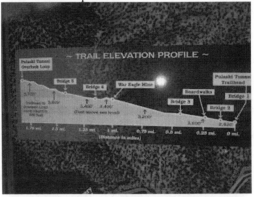

I hiked in front and George followed. I kept my ears tuned in to his footsteps. His coordination stayed good.

The Pulaski trail signs tell a story of Fireman Pulaski and the 1910 fire. It is an incredible story of survival, heroism and destruction.

A major multi-year drought combined with gale-force winds..."The energy released by the fire during the firestorm equaled that produced by WWII size atomic bombs..."

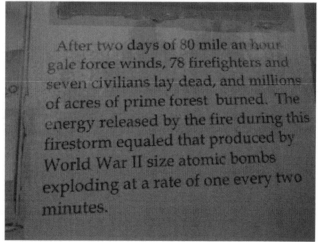

After two days of 80 mile an hour gale force winds, 78 firefighters and seven civilians lay dead, and millions of acres of prime forest burned. The energy released by the fire during this firestorm equaled that produced by World War II size atomic bombs exploding at a rate of one every two minutes.

Each kiosk displayed the Pulaski tool that the fireman created to help fight fires. It is still used by fire-fighters today.

Our legs became soaked with cold rain from brushing against plants.

About five years ago we had done this trail with our friends, Regis and Cindy Hampton. I kept having memories of them, their black lab (who was quite old at the time) zig-zagging down to the creek that runs next to the trail and back up the hill. The dog had high-energy and was agile for an old dog. Like Regis (60-plus years old) who sometimes ran with the dog up and down the steep slopes.

At the overlook to the tunnel there is a stone wall. We could see a small tunnel opening from where we stood by the wall. Pulaski had to threaten to shoot the men he had saved from the fire if they tried to dash out of the tunnel. You can imagine the panic as smoke and heat entered the cave. All the men suffered from burns and passed out.

At the top of our hike we stopped and munched on our pistachios. We started to get cold. Even with the raincoats we felt damp and cold.

George walked very well. It wasn't until the last three-quarter of a mile that he stumbled once. I noticed he was starting to lean toward the right.

We stopped on a bridge, and I hugged him and he was shivering. When I pulled away, he looked down and he was wetting his pants. But the solution to the urge or to what was happening didn't click in him. I said, "Go over here and go potty."

He did. It surprises me. I don't know if it surprises him.

This incontinence comes with the loss of brain. For now it doesn't happen very often, but four miles of walking can, I suppose, tire out his brain.

When we get to the car, I see it is 46 degrees. I blast the heat and George thinks to wait for a towel for the seat before getting into the car. "He is aware," I think.

This is the thing. I want to tell our journey through this illness. But I want to respect this man that I love. George was neat and clean, responsible and organized all his life. I fear that he might have a good day and read this and be hurt that I would tell the story of his loss of bladder control. I don't want this telling to be an insult to this man or those who love him, like our children.

As I write this my eyes fill with tears.

It is part of the journey we both are on.

I drive down into Wallace and I stop at a grocery to get some soup to heat in our room for lunch. I ask George if he wants to stay in the car and wait. (Since he seemed aware his pants are wet with urine a few minutes ago.) But he wants to come in. Wet pants didn't bother him; I don't remind him.

I asked him what to eat with the soup.

He says, "Fritos."

Good idea.

I worked in the afternoon on my job as an assistant to a small business owner. Cold and rainy, a good day to stay inside.

In the evening I found "Men in Black" on the TV. We don't get TV at home. Sometimes in a motel we will watch. This was a treat. We had to endure lots of commercials, but we sat in the bed propped up on pillows and watched it all the way to the end.

Lovely Trike Ride

Day 35 we bike the Coeur d'lene Trail again.

We stop on a bridge where a couple is watching their dog have fun in the river. He swims up and down stream and every once in a while he jumps and splashes. It makes us smile.

When it was lunch time, we found a pretty spot on the trail and turned our bikes sideways.

NO MOOSE SIGHTINGS! We saw:

A deer

A coyote puppy

A blue heron that launched into flight and left a looooong stream of poop

A dead mouse...

52 miles of riding.   There was left over pizza and salad in our room. And Dove dark chocolates...

I was able to find a place to stay before we reach Portland before George started standing and hovering. "You want to go for a walk?" I asked.

We were on the move again.

Tomorrow we leave this lovely trail. I ask George if we should reserve a room for next year's TOT.

He grinned real big.

Day 36 - Amazing Roads and Folks

I hate traveling by car... at least I did, until today. We had an awesome travel day.

At the motel checkout I said I would like to reserve our room for TOT next year. (It will cost me $28 to cancel if it turns out we can't do it, so why not try?)

On the road we headed west on Interstate 90. The clouds hanging low over the mountains.

Our time was now going to be constricted by a date we have to be in Colorado to meet up with my brother.

I turned off the highway to get gas. The gas station had some old phone booths... minus the phones but still with the phone books.

As we had turned into the gas station, I had seen a sign for a bike trail I thought we might try today. I was unsure because I didn't know what kind of surface it had.

I followed the signs to the trail on a lightly traveled road.

I turned onto a gravel road to get to a place where we could get on the trail.

The trail surface was way too rough for our trikes.

I programmed the iPad to take us to Kennewick and avoid highways.

In real short order I stopped the van and ran back to take a picture of a sign we had just passed.

137

See the chicken scratches for the population count?

The town was maybe two blocks long in either direction. It had a couple of grain elevators, houses and a church.

After Lamont we passed lots of grain fields, some green and most golden.

Then the road became gravel.

I love it. No traffic, I could stop anywhere, take pictures, yell. I kissed George. Smiles!

Just before we reached a place where I turned off the gravel road I noticed a car behind me. It was a sheriff's car. I thought, with Lamont so small, someone probably alerted the sheriff that there were strangers in town.

After lunch we were back on a highway to Kennewick, WA.

They water the grass and the plants at the wayside. Everywhere else the grasses were brown.

I called our host for the night and he offered some ideas and places in Kennewick for us to see/do.

An area of downtown Richland has shops, an art gallery, a bike shop and a park on the river.

George and I played the xylophone together. It really had a nice sound. I could get into playing that. It didn't keep George's interest.

The playground had other cool stuff. And the whole park was very busy with families.

I stuck my feet in the water. It was cool and refreshing. I said to George, "Come try it." I didn't expect him to. He hasn't played in water in years.

But he did!

Our Affordable Travel Club hosts are absolutely wonderful. They put out some crackers and cheese and shared some wine with us when we arrived.

Bill works with wood and his partner made these wine stoppers.

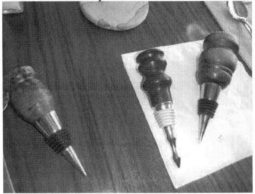

They have done a lot of traveling. Bill put on a video of an art event. An old limestone mine left nice walls, so an artist put a slide show together and displayed it on the walls of the mine.

Bill has created lovely wooden sliders for in front of his TV.

I was hesitating about drinking my second glass of wine, and Bill offered to drive us and go with us to the restaurant. Cool!

We went to a Mexican restaurant.

Dinner was good and our hosts had some great stories to share about business and travel.

They told us about the Mary Hill Museum on Hwy 14. It is about three hours to Mt. Hood. We head that way tomorrow.

George's and my dinner came to under $20 with tip. Smiles.

Later, George had something to throw away. So I took him into the bathroom and showed him the waste basket. Back in the bedroom, right away he wanted to brush his teeth and got his toothbrush ready but didn't know where to go to brush his teeth. I took him to the bathroom again.

We went for a walk. When we got back I told George to go to the bathroom before he got undressed for bed. I had to show him where the bathroom was again. A good thing is that he has no sadness about the decline in ability. He seems to be happy. That is such a blessing.

Day 37 – Miles of Smiles

June 27, 2016 was a full day of smiles and miles of travel.

I worked a bit in the morning and when I went out to the dining room, George and our hosts were already dining on breakfast. I was a bit embarrassed. I was so involved in my work I didn't even hear what was happening in the next room

Verna had made us a wonderful breakfast including nectarines that came from their own tree.

Bill had some more great stories to tell at breakfast. His email statements below his signature give you an idea of his humor.

"Everything happens for a reason, sometimes it's because you are stupid and make bad decisions."

"A recent study has found that women who carry a little extra weight live longer than men who mention it."

I felt honored to be their guests. I love these travel clubs!

George hugged our hosts and off we went in the car, heading west.

Right away as we left Kennewick we started ascending out of the river valley into golden grass-covered hills. In the far-off haze we could see a snow-covered mountain -- Mount Hood in Oregon

The Columbia River has created a passageway through hills and mountains. Roads, rails, and power lines follow that natural path.

George said, "That island looks like a submarine."

I was wondering when we would ever see a gas station.

Verna had told us about a Stonehenge replica on Hwy 14.

I found a gas station. This gas station had character.

I peeked in the box and giggled. I told George, "It is baby rattles." I giggled. "I have to get my camera."

I went to the car, got the camera and came back and George was still bent over the box trying to find the snakes.

I guess I wasn't explaining it right. I tried telling him. Then I said, "Toy rattles for babies."

"Oh!" he said.

Here are some more pictures from the gas station.

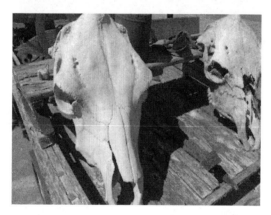

Verna also told us about the Mary Hill museum. We stopped there and first toured the art outside.

Inside the museum we watched a video on creating the first paved road up the Columbia River. Sam Hill paid for it himself after failing to get the government to pay. It cost him $100,000.

At the museum café we had veggie sandwiches on a patio overlooking the river.

I said to George, "We are driving through this beautiful tapestry of nature, and we stop at a building that is a work of art and is surrounded by pieces of art and holds art, and I am taking pictures of it which could be called art. It is all very..... artistic."

We cross the river on the Hood Bridge. It is an old, iron, NARROW bridge.

Off to our right I when we were on the bridge I saw lots of colorful kites. After the bridge I turned in to find them.

The boards have boots attached. When this guy took off zooming over the water his excited dog followed swimming. The surfer went to the other side of a bay and the dog got up on land there and then ran back and forth down the beach as the guy surfed back and forth just off shore.

153

As we stood watching with big smiles on our faces, a surfer came to shore by us. He looked like he came right off the cover of a romance novel. "It really is as fun as it looks," he said to us. He exchanged his board that had the boots attached with just a flat board and took off again.

From where we were it was a one hour drive to get to Timberline Lodge on Hood Mountain. (Mt. Hood). We started the drive up.

The last couple curves were nerve racking. I was glad when we parked at the lodge and began moving around on foot.

Snow!

Back down the mountain we stopped at a grocery store in White Salmon, Washington. WOW! It was like a Trader Joe's! That is amazing for a small town. We got some salads from the deli and set off to find our host's home.

When we arrived our hostess was watering her beautiful flower gardens. She took us through the guest cottage (where we will stay). Oh my! It is so roomy.

Then she took us on our tour of the big house. Her windows are overlooking the beach where we watched the wind surfers earlier today!

Below is a picture I took from the beach. See the brown house on the cliff in the picture? It is a house under construction near her house.

We didn't get around to eating our deli salads until 9:00 p.m. What a full day with lots of beauty and fun.

Tomorrow I haven't a clue of what we will do. I just know that at the end of this big day I am too tired to plan.

The Exercises

Some of the readers of this blog who have spouses with Alzheimer's and Parkinson's have asked me to give more information about our exercises.

These exercises were designed specifically for what the Qigong Massage guy observed while watching George. They may not work for you or your person. George was tight in the calves, hips and chest and needed to stretch those, and he needed to do cross the body exercises. (Right arm – left leg, left arm – right leg). These will keep those pathways in his brain working and will help to keep him mobile longer.

- Chicken Breathing
- Elbow to opposite knee
- Walk and punch
- Model walk
- Sobriety test walk
- Tiny Grapevine
- Walk on your heels
- Twist arm swing

Chicken breathing

Oh boy, how do I explain the chicken? It is a breathing exercise that practices a slight undulation of the spine.

Starting on the end of the out-breath the top of the pelvis tilts backward slightly (gently moving the pubic bone forward). Do this without squeezing the buns; the lower abdominal muscles do the work. On a slow in-breath the arms move up in front of you to about shoulder height with palms up, then sweep out to the side palms forward. As you are bringing the arms out to the side, bring the shoulder blades together and expand the chest in front and tuck in the chin. The tuck moves the whole head back a small distance. You are not moving the chin down. The jaw line stays parallel to the floor. Think of a pin poking your chin. If you think of a chicken bringing his head back to get ready to peck something you can see what I mean...hence the "chicken" name. Relax slowly with the exhale and turn the hands down towards the floor and bring them together as if holding a ball just in front of your pubic bone. In Qigong that is a ball of energy you are holding.

At the end of the exhale the pelvis tilts to hold two seconds. Repeat.

Work to make this all a smooth lovely movement without jerks or effort. It takes a lot of practice to get to that point. Work up to 30 breaths.

Elbow to opposite knee

The next few exercises were designed to get George doing things to move across his body -- to twist his spine which he doesn't do very well. In this standing exercise the left knee comes up, and the right elbow reaches for the left knee. Put the left foot back down on the ground and lift the right knee. The left elbow reaches for the right knee. Put the right foot back on the ground. Repeat.

Walk and punch

Walk so that when the left leg goes forward, the right arm punches forward. Then right leg, left arm. George would lose form after only about 3 repetitions. This one was hard for him.

Model walk

Think of a model, standing tall, chin in (chicken) and chest out. Left leg steps forward crossing over the center to the right, and right shoulder moves forward at the same time. Then right leg steps forward crossing slightly to the the left of the body's center line and left shoulder moves forward. It is a kind of twisting of the spine side to side as you walk.

Sobriety test walk

Walk a straight line of baby steps. See it pictured below. Right heels just in front of the left toes.

Tiny grapevines

Cross the right leg over the left, and put your right foot down next to your left foot, so that the outsides of the feet are touching each other. Then take your left foot and uncross and set the foot next to the right, so the insides of the feet are touching each other. Keep doing this so the sides of your feet touch each other each time. Do about ten and then change direction.

Walk on your heels

Lift your toes off the ground and walk on your heels.

Day 38 - 39

Beautiful White Salmon

We are so grateful for our Affordable Travel Club host, Peyt, who let us just "hang out" in and around the guest house today. After 37 days of travel and small rooms, it was great to be in this guest cottage on a cliff overlooking the Columbia River Gorge. We feel so blessed and surrounded by beauty and kindness.

I had been so tired the night before; I didn't get a chance to upload the day's pictures to the blog. I got that going this morning. It takes a while.

We went for a walk.

We walked around downtown and later we found a nice restaurant with green salads, veggie omelets and even veggie sausage patties.

Back at our cottage we sat on a bench that overlooks the gorge.

Peyt wanted to take us for a ride to show us some of the area. She is quite an interesting lady. She has sailed half way around the world, organized the local parade and traveled extensively starting as a teenager.

She took us through the industrial park.

She told us the story of Insitu. A few young men started Insitu and in less than 10 years sold it to Boeing for a few billion.

The town used to be farmers and fishermen in flannel shirts. Now it's young families with money. Ahhh! That explains the trendy grocery and the vegetarian sausage.

She drove us over the bridge to a bike trail she knew about. She didn't know how long the trail was.

I asked Peyt about all the flags on her porch.

She said they are the flags of every country that she has visited.

The pine trees leave pitch on the bottoms of our shoes. I leave them outside. But then I run to the car to get something and I have pitch on my bare feet -- so much for saving the floors.

We sat out overlooking the Columbia River Gorge until George got up and said, "Mosquitos are out."

I heard one of Peyt's cats howling in the garage. When I opened the door to the garage I found he had left us a present. A dead mouse... or mole. Thank you!

ALZHEIMER'S TRIPPIN' with George

New Brain Loss Symptoms

We are always moving -- whether it is on our bikes or in a car or on our feet. Sometimes the moving is from one stage to another -- from denial to acceptance, from independence to dependence...

We started out **Day 39** by doing our exercises by the cliff, and then we were hungry so we knocked on our host's door. She swung the door wide and welcomed us in with a big smile. How nice is that!

Peyt put George to work chopping onions, and I went to work making coffee. Peyt put out a nice spread.

She dined with us and the conversation flowed wonderfully.

Later I drove to the trail that Peyt had shown us yesterday.

It was very windy. I asked another couple that was just starting their ride how long the trail was. They said nine miles round trip.

It was a WONDERFUL short ride.

At the start of the trail was a visitor's center. Of course it was closed.

I studied the map to find another trail. I found one that I thought might work. It was 30 minutes away, starting at the Bridge of the Gods.

We were supposed to be back at the house and ready to go with Peyt to a music concert in another town at around 5:00 pm. I figured we could get a couple hours of biking in before we had to head home to shower.

I saw a sign for the ANTIQUE AIRPLANE AND AUTO MUSEUM. I asked George if he wanted to go.

He is/was a mechanical kind of guy and loves old cars. He said "Yes."

We got down the first aisle and George needed to find a bathroom. I led him back to the entrance where the restrooms were.

There weren't just cars and airplanes there. There were motorcycles, bicycles and wheelchairs. There were cameras and telephones and wagons. There were lots of videos. We watched one on Wilber and Orville Wright. It was interesting, but long.

169

Then we started looking at stuff and passed several other videos. I said we would never get through the museum if we didn't stop watching videos.

I asked George which car thrilled him the most. And he said, "They all do." I was glad we took the time to go to the museum.

George pointed at the rear of this bike. I said, "Yes, it looks like it got bent up pretty good." Then he stuttered and said, "Gear drive, there is no chain."

Oh ya!

The founder offered to take our pictures in the corvette.

George was losing interest. We left the museum and headed back to a café we had passed, the "GOOD NEWS GARDEN and CAFÉ".

I decide we have time to at least look at the other trail we were aiming for.

The trail head is close to the Bridge of the Gods. I looked for information about why this place was called "Bridge of the Gods." I found none.

We walked down the trail.

I assembled this man and took his picture and I thought it would make George smile at my silliness. It didn't. I learned later why he wasn't responding as expected.

When we got back to the car, there were no bathrooms. I mentioned that to George. As we were getting into the car George looked down at himself. "Do you need to go pee?" I asked.

He nodded. I said, well come on, there are bushes over here. So we walked a few feet down the trail, and I stood guard while he relieved himself.

We got back in the car and traveled the bridge over the Columbia River to Washington.

Right after the bridge I saw a historical marker sign and pulled in and found a porta-potty for me to use.

I read the kiosk and it explained the name of Bridge of the Gods. It came from a Native American story that at one time their people could walk across the river on rocks in that location. Geologists have confirmed that this Native American story actually occurred. A landslide actually happened that was big enough to block the river....

When I got back to the car, George was gone. I was surprised that he needed to use the porta-potty since he had just urinated on the other side of the bridge.

When he got back in the car he brought an odor with him.

I didn't beat around the bush or criticize. I think I did well. I said, "I smell poop. Did you have an accident?"

George said, "I had an accident."

I touched his head and said, "If you can tell me you need a bathroom I will try real hard to find one for you. You need to tell me if you can."

He nodded.

We got back to the cottage it was ten minutes to 5:00. We were supposed to be ready at 5:00 to go with Peyt.

George was already in the bathroom when I got into the cottage. I offered help, he didn't want any.

Soon he opened the door all dressed and ready to go. He had rinsed out the clothes well... I double checked.

But I told him go back in and take a shower.

Bossing him around like this is new to both of us.

George is out of the shower and cleaned up. I hug him. Then I hear Peyt. It is time to go she says and she heads for her BMW in the garage.

I look at George and now the front of his shorts is wet... Another accident!

A quick change, I grab a towel for the evening and worry he will have an issue in her BMW.

Peyt takes us for a lovely ride through the countryside away from the gorge.

She takes us to a very small town, Glenwood.

Yet the restaurant had veggie burgers. All we saw in town was a few houses, a park, the General Store, and the restaurant.

In the park was a concert.

Each of us was to go up and pick a song. I picked "Five Foot Two" and "The Green Green Grass of Home." Someone else chose "King of the Road."

There were about 20 folks there. Afterward they served watermelon.

Back at the house, Peyt wanted to make us breakfast tomorrow, and I wanted to get an early start. She didn't want us to go without making us breakfast. She made breakfast to go. I gave her some containers to put it into. When I took the containers to her, she asked about George. He was in the cottage and we were in the house, so we could talk about him.

I had already told her and she had already sensed and witnessed George's loss in cognition. But I told her about the incontinent moments we were experiencing...

She hugged me. She was very sweet. She wants to help. She has helped herself with some alternative healing practices.

176

She has a way of asking a "higher power/God/Guardian Angel/whatever you want to call it" for guidance. "Do I need this?" and she gets an answer.

I went and got George, and she tried to teach it to George. She was hoping this might help stop, slow, or reverse his illness. We didn't see any action when George did it.

Anyway, we talked for maybe five minutes after George returned to the cottage. When I entered the cottage George was standing in the living room near the door... facing the door...just standing there. I asked if he was going outside.

"No," he said.

"What are you doing?" I ask.

"I don't know," he said.

I think this is the day had been extremely fun and different. I did not get to sleep until after 2:00 a.m.

Pictures of George's Brain

Some caregivers get impatient with their loved one's incontinence. They are blaming the victim in a sense, as if they were messing their pants on purpose.

Here is George's reality in pictures. This is a scan of a healthy brain.

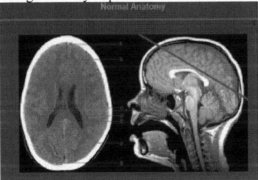

Below is a scan of George's brain taken over one-year ago.

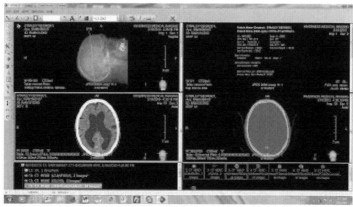

A very large hole in the middle of his brain has formed.

A PET scan of his brain activity showed diminished capacity on the left side of his brain, hence, planning ahead, strategic thinking is harmed. A positive is that he is less critical of things. He has lost language and gained singing... THAT makes for more fun.

What amazes me is that so many times he returns and talks and seems to think like he used to. His voice and laugh returns to normal. How can that be???

Day 40 - OH JOY, the Pacific!

In the morning George sat down with a book while I packed! It went well!

We avoided the interstate and opted to drive the slower, less congested highway that runs along the Columbia River.

Our picnic today was lovely. Peyt had given us spinach and blueberries and I made a salad for each of us. She also gave us egg salad. Yum!

Peyt had told us about a tower/column in Astoria with paintings on the walls. We were going through Astoria, WA. I made the tower our destination.

I had expected the painting to be on the inside of the tower and that you look at the paintings as you climb the stairs to the top. But the paintings were on the outside of the tower, they were about Lewis and Clark and the settling of the area by the Euro-Americans.

I walked with George around the tower trying to read the inscription. But the reading was very slow. Blah blah blah........blah.......blah blah.... George was laughing.

But on the second trip around he said, "I am going in." I went one more round, got b   met him at the top.

Thank you, Peyt, for the suggestion.

I tried a selfie.

We are staying at the Mermaid Motel in Long Beach. $77 senior rate. The owner is delightful and told us about a paved bike trail along the dunes by the beach.

What a fun trail!!!! Curves and tiny hills are so fun on a trike. We didn't even know about this trail.

It is only six miles.

Is that a whale bone? I touch it. YES! It is a bone!

On November 19, 1805
Capt. William Clark
led a small party
along this beach.
This excursion was
their first contact
with the Pacific Ocean.

After dinner we drove down to the south end of the beach where the owner of the motel said there were less people. I optimistically decided to walk to the rocky hillside to the south.

We had to walk across a stream so I had George take his tennis shoes off. He was walking barefoot. We had to keep a close eye out for jelly fish washed up on the sand. There were A LOT!!

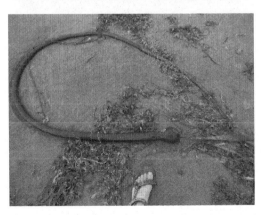

It seemed like the hills were so close, but we walked and walked and walked.

Finally we made it to the rocks. YEAH!

Now we have to walk back....

Over two hours of walking on sand. My hips and feet ached. Poor George!

Tomorrow we head to Portland to stay with Sylvia.

We are excited to be seeing her and finally visiting Portland.

You may be wondering why we aren't seeing more of Washington and Oregon. Why are we leaving the beach so soon?

This journey started out with us just visiting Madison, Wisconsin and Colorado. When the Madison Airbnb canceled, I decided we would go to Idaho for the TOT and then since we are so close let's go to Portland and while we are that close...

But we have a deadline to be in Colorado. We have to keep moving...

Day 41 - Portland and Repeats

July 1, 2016, it's my birthday. First thing, I checked my email and found I no longer had a job. The work had been getting less and less, and now I was not needed. I look to the bright side. This change frees me up to enjoy this trip and George.

Today we traveled back south toward Portland, Oregon. It occurred to me that we were now going toward our home in Florida instead of away from it.

Maybe this concept was why I was feeling unenthusiastic and worn out.

On the way to the Pacific there was a stretch of road where I couldn't stop yawning. I had rolled the windows down but still could not stop. On the way back now, in the same area it happened again. What's up with that?

It didn't take long to get to Portland and Sylvia's. She is house-sitting for a college-friend's mother.

A great place to stay near uptown Portland with its yoga studios, trendy shops and big old homes mixed with modern condos built into the hillsides.

The porch on the house where we are staying overlooks Portland. We can see two mountains from the balcony; Mt. St. Helen and Mt. Adams.

We went for a walk. And the tired/down feeling that was with me today lifted. Exercise and sunshine are anti-depressants.

We crossed a bridge over a railway and a road. People used to jump off it to commit suicide, so the city put up a fence and a sign saying "We can help you cross the bridge" and a phone number.

Sylvia pointed out this redwood tree as we passed.

Sylvia took us into a shop selling Himalayan Salt. Sylvia told of a place in her travels where they had rooms filled with salt and you lay in them and the salt warmed you up.

Back at Sylvia's home I caught up on email. Sylvia made us all great salads and a stir fry.

We sat around the dining room table afterward with our iPads and computers. George mentioned to Sylvia that we used to do a lot of work for John Deere (through the business we owned.) A few minutes later he said it again. Then a few minutes later he said, "We had a guy that worked for us, and we used to do a lot of work for John Deere. And the guy went to work for John Deere."

Sylvia asked if the guy still worked there.

George looked at me. He didn't know! Then we went out on the balcony to sit and George repeated the story again.

Sylvia and I looked at each other.

This repeating is common in dementia patients. It is a new behavior in George. It is new to me tonight.

I wonder how we will stay with strangers through the Evergreen Club and Affordable Travel Club if he starts doing this often.

I now include a short paragraph and tell potential hosts, "He is sweet and quiet and doesn't wander yet. He was a genius at programming and engineering."

Day 42 -44 Joys of Staying with Sylvia

July 2, 2016, Sylvia had suggested we all go to the Farmers' Market on Saturday morning. Sylvia wasn't around when we got up. We could walk there, she had told me. I looked it up on the iPad and mapped our route. Less than a mile! Easy-peasy.

At the farmers' market the vendors were still setting up.

We found an open coffee vendor. We sat on a bench and drank our coffees and then I remembered that it is later in the morning back in Wisconsin and Illinois. I called our kids! I'd chat for a while and then pass the phone over to George. He was able to say things and carry on a good conversation with them.

The Farmer's Market opened at 8:30. I texted Sylvia and let her know where we were. She said she'd walk down and join us.

We tried the lavender infused jams. We bought the pear-fig jam.

I picked out some pumpkin seed butter and Sylvia joined us and said she had gotten the walnut butter and it was good. The vendor said, "That's the brain butter."

"Brain Butter? We need that!" I got the walnut butter too.

and onions

and chard.

We saw such beautiful produce and people!

Our bags full we walked back up the hillside.

Later Sylvia offered to show us around Portland by trike. I was excited to get a tour of some of the (famous among bicycle advocates) bike lanes and trails in and around the city of Portland.

Portland has buses and trolleys and passenger trains and more....

Down by the river there are some people living in tents. I'd call them homeless, but they have a tent. Portland or someone provided them a porta-john. They have a tent home on the river.

The trail runs right by several homeless "communities." In one spot there were about 20 tents lining the trail. Some had taken rocks to define their "yards" and "pathways" One had mulch spread on their entryway path.

Two men were standing on the path, and I got kind of nervous. One was holding clubs or something in each of his hands. As we passed I saw that one of the objects was a very large knife. Like a machete. I peddled faster for a while, leaving Sylvia and George behind.

Sometimes there was no tent. A couple might be sorting through their pile of stuff under a bridge.

If there was no porta-john in the area then often times as we approached a homeless couple or individual we got whiffs of human feces.... or au d'pooh as they say in France.

Sylvia said that there was a rise recently in the number of homeless. She thinks it was due to the rise in housing prices, both to buy and rent. So many people live pay-check to pay-check. It doesn't take much, a job loss, a rise in rent without a rise in pay, or an illness. Then they find themselves in a desperate situation.

Sylvia took us down to the Columbia River. In the distance we could see Mt. Hood.

We rode 36 miles.

While George showered, I created a stir-fry with some of those farmers' market veggies.

After dinner while I showered, did laundry and checked email and uploaded pictures, George sat out on the deck.

Day 43 was another great day with Sylvia in Portland, Oregon.

Sylvia drove us through town to a huge park to hike with some friends of hers.

Some of her friends we had already met at the Trike event in Kellogg, Idaho last week. Barbara has an Elf, a unique trike in a shell.

Before we took off walking, I tried to get a group picture, but everyone was chatting and greeting each other. All the best groups are like this.

199

From the park, we got some nice views of the city.

George did great and kept up with the group.

At one point we decided to take some stairs down the hill. It is like going down seven flights of steep stairs. I got down and turned around to see how George was doing. He was doing great, but he was looking at me looking at him and I think it messed him up. I could see his right foot and leg were not following commands from the brain smoothly... hesitating and shaking.

I said, "Hang on George!" He was looking at me and began to lean back more and more. (Leaning back is good when you are going down stairs. At least if you slip you sit down instead of tumble forward.)

The last few steps were very slow, but he made it and then I had him stretch out his calves and his thighs.

The next set of stairs was only two flights and he hopped down them just fine. Weird.

After our walk we got a big table at the coffee shop. It was so great to chat with everyone.

George and I rested and Sylvia went to the airport to pick up another guest she had met on one of her trike tours. This woman, April, is a Warmshowers host in Connecticut.

After lunch we walked to the Rose Garden and Japanese Garden. They are right next to each other.

Pretty impressive.

The rose garden was free. There was a small fee for the Japanese Garden. April paid for it! Thank you, April!

Sylvia said the benches are placed strategically to give you an artistic view when you sit there. She likes to sit on each bench and soak in the scene.

The garden was very busy. At one point we sat on a bench and watched the fashion show go by. George said, "I love to watch people."

On the way back we were walking down down down a hill on the sidewalk and right next to us a skateboarder had to put his skateboard sideways and skid to avoid colliding with a car that pulled out in front of him. He had crouched low and used a gloved hand to assist in the breaking.

Amazing! He just flipped his board straight, got back on and continued down the hill. I took a picture of the skid marks.

After another amazing stir-fry dinner made with more of the veggies we got at the farmer's market, I drove to get some desperately needed supplies.

Day 44, July 4th, I ended the day standing in the living room and saying, "This is one of the most amazing experiences of my life!"

That is how the day ended.

A bike ride on the Banks-Vernonia Trail is how the day started. It is about 25 minutes west of Portland.

The parking lot was full! Oh yes, Sunday and a holiday weekend, we aren't the only ones with this idea.

Sylvia said there were lots of blackberries on the trail. "Take a container," she said. So I did.

We got a few, but in a week or two the bushes will be loaded.

I had learned on our walk yesterday that blackberries are an invasive species here. It was evident that they were taking over parts of the trail. The trail goes right through a free-range farm.

The trail traverses through gorgeous forests, the trees covered in mosses, the ground covered in ferns.

At one point on the trail it descends by switch backs. Sylvia had warned us, and a good thing too. There are no signs warning of the sharp turns.

I fed this sheep a flower.

In Vernonia we had our picnic lunch at a park by the river.

We had PB&J and oranges for lunch. Then we went to the market and picked up popcorn and chocolate.

The guy at the counter said, "You guys are so orange, you have orange shirts and I smell oranges!"

Twenty minutes later I thought, "And we are from Florida!"

Back at the farm the ducks and chickens and turkeys were on the trail.

The farmer was out. She was letting bikers hold the baby goat.

We went home, and Sylvia and I whipped up an amazing sweet potato soup and fruit salad.

While the soup was cooking, I took George out on the deck, and we did his exercises. The deck looks over Portland and beyond. It was amazing to be scooping up energy from this beautiful location.

The night before the food was so beautiful that Sylvia and I put both arms up and said "YEAAAAAH." That's an amazing grace. We did it again this night... joyful over good food and good company.

Joining us this evening were Sylvia's friends, Annie and April. We had a mini party for our 4th of July.

After dinner I checked email, and there was an email from a friend whose husband is showing dementia symptoms. She said he recently began to leave his Depends pads out to dry so the house is beginning to smell like urine. She has to use special soap to get the smell out of the clothes. Sigh... I wonder if a special soap is needed for George's clothes.

As it got dark we started seeing fireworks set off by communities, neighborhoods and individuals. We could see a line of them all along the horizon.

Right across the Columbia River, in Washington fireworks are allowed. They are not allowed in Oregon. Hence the line of flashing lights on the opposite side of the river. I was filled with joy and awe. That is when I said it. "This is one of the most amazing experiences of my life!"

Smiles.

Day 45 – 46 - Crater Lake Area

We had such a great time with Sylvia that we were sorry to leave. I wrote her a note. Other than Facebook and her website, I wonder if I will see her again.

We passed a covered bridge early in the day. I stopped at the next one I saw and learned that this area has a lot of covered bridges.

We were hungry, but finding a place open and able to serve vegetarians was a challenge. Then I saw that DQ had a sign, they serve breakfast!

George was happy.

The tourist magazine showed there were a lot of sites to see in the area. Cascade lakes, volcanos, waterfalls, overlooks....

We stopped at Salt Creek Falls.

Black swifts nest behind the falls, having one nestling at a time and only feeding it twice a day.

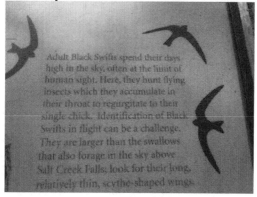

We walked to the falls, and then George wanted his camera. We walked back to the car and got his camera.

We arrived at our motel in Crestview, Oregon around 2:00 p.m. The motel and town appears to be mostly for hunters and fishermen.

Across the street they sell booze and guns.

We took it for two nights at $55 per night.

After we checked in we found that the internet doesn't reach our room. I have to sit outside by the office in the cold if I want to upload pictures to this blog.

After the long drive we needed to walk. The town was pretty small and soon the street was dirt, and then two-track. I had google-mapped our route but without street signs and gravel roads turning to dirt... after a couple turns....

I decided to start marking our walk in case we had to turn around and come back this way. The marker below was on the right side of the road. "Take the second right" was my message.

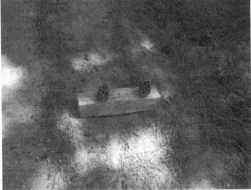

Smiles... but George was nervous, and I was too. A few months ago we got lost on a trail. I made a bad slideshow/video about it and put it on Youtube. If you watch it, fast forward through the boring parts. Today I was afraid of a repeat in this vast wilderness. We turned around.

I was anxious to see Crater Lake which other travelers had told us was something we shouldn't miss. Already it was 3:30 and Crater Lake was over 45 minutes away. I decided to go anyway rather than sit in our little room.

It was windy and cold up at Crater Lake!

See the girl's hair blowing in the wind (below)?

All the information offices were closed.

On the way back to our motel I saw these clouds.

I am already missing being around people and socializing.

On **Day 46** we went to the La Pine visitors' center. Good idea! The volunteer was helpful and pointed us in the direction of Newberry National Volcanic Monument. She said there would be short trails for interesting hikes.

George's National Park Senior Pass worked to get us in free.

After the falls we found the visitors center, and again good information. She told us of several short hikes to do. She said a hike around the small crater would give us a good view of the larger crater.

What??? It turns out that like Crater Lake, this was a big mountain of lava and the top caved in forming a lake. Then a few other volcanos happened, splitting the lake in two. Those volcanos also collapsed.

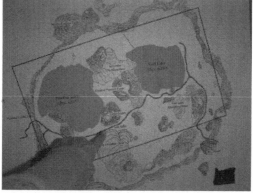

Our first stop was the Obsidian Flow. I had no idea what an obsidian flow was. This would be educational.

As we were walking through the woods on the trail I looked to the right and there was this HUGE pile of black rock. Like a mining site.

Obsidian is glass with a bit of metal in it to give it a dark color. It was a valuable rock for the natives that used the glass rock for tools.

The path took us right up onto the pile. A sign warned not to take pets or wear sandals because we would be actually walking on pieces of glass.

Some areas were quite rocky to walk on and at one place we had to climb down over some rocks. I had to instruct George on where to place his foot and where to place his hand to hold on. It hits me that he doesn't bend over very well or squat very good anymore. He is getting so stiff!

Frogs on the flow??? Yes, they come by the thousands in August.

I chose to walk the trail to the hot springs, which would be pretty flat along the shore of the lake.

There were pretty rocks and pretty mosses.

We stopped and had our picnic lunch sitting on the ground.

I kept listening for George to stumble or stub his toe. The path had lots of roots and rocks that we had to step over and manipulate around. He never stumbled!

Toward the end of our walk I took pictures of the path to show you how rough it was. I felt I walked slower than I normally would have due to my concerns. But even so, as I was walking along I was thinking, "Gee, he has to think to turn his foot to fit here, step high enough over that."

Yes, we walked across the rocks below as part of the path.

After that I drove us back to town to use the library and do laundry in La Pine. I took George over to the laundromat and started a load and had him sit there with his book, while I went to the library to work on stuff. I was nervous about leaving him there alone.

When I got back to the laundromat, George was filling the dryer with the wet clothes. The attendant came over and said, "We have a policy of not leaving your children unattended here."

My eyes must have gotten big with worry about what had happened. Then she laughed, "Just kidding!"

Now to DQ for blizzard time!

We had some dear friends that were about to close on the sale of their business. George and I had sold a business once and we knew how very stressful the whole process can be. So we clicked our cups in honor of our friends. Here's to a smooth closing and a great new stage of life!

Day 47 - 49 Drive and Drive and Drive

It was a foggy cool morning and thirty-four degrees.

We stopped for gas in Bend, Oregon. We had heard it was a neat and trendy place. I saw what people were talking about. There was a dispenser for kombucha in the gas station!

Kombucha is a fermented tea used as a probiotic. This dispenser is an indicator that the area residents are health conscious.

Fun bathroom signs.

Oregon requires gas to be dispensed by a professional. At this station a guy dressed the part with white shorts, white shirt, and a white hat.

After that stop we had miles of wide-open spaces.

After an hour or two we stopped at a wayside and did our exercises.

George was doing well enough today to get bored by the long drive on flat open spaces. He thought to get his iPad and a book out of his bag.

In Boise our travel club hosts Debbie and Mike sat and chatted with us out in the shade on their back porch. They gave us directions to a place to walk. I also asked for a place to get the oil changed and the car washed. Mike drew me a nice map.

The bike path in Boise runs on both sides of the river. We walked a loop.

Then we drove up the hill to a park to watch the sky as the sun set. It is a wetland and there were lots of ducks.

I said, "Look, a dead duck!" It hit me as funny and we both laughed and laughed.

Day 48 had some frustrating turn-around moments. I used the map that our hosts had drawn for us the previous evening to change the oil in our car.

Our hosts had told us to get off on Hwy 30. A beautiful drive and you will go by Thousand Springs which had water shooting out of the cliffs from underground rivers. Doesn't that sound cool??

I used a map we picked up at a visitors center to find my exit.

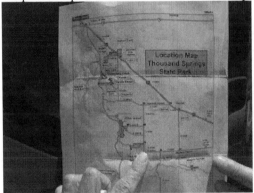

I was on Hwy 84. After several turn arounds I asked some young people in a wayside about a Thousand Springs. They were full of piercings. One girl covered up her face to talk to me. ??? Is she hiding all her piercings? She must have had 7 to 12 in her face.

They had never heard of a Thousand Springs. They went back to looking at their phones.

I might have missed a turn. I had no cell service so I couldn't use Google.

I turn around and retrace our drive several more times.

Finally I get on Highway 30 but each time I think I find the park, it is dead end.

I know I am making this harder than it should be.

Now I am getting grumpy and frustrated. George is being very patient. I try using all the gizmos to find the springs. No luck. .

Heck with it! I use our navigator to get to our next destination.

Later I follow the signs to a visitor center and find our way to different water falls after only a few turn-arounds.

We were there with a LOT of other travelers.

Back in the car I found a route off the Interstate.

We stopped at a gas station. These dogs were waiting for their master inside a restaurant.

Back roads, wide open spaces. Loved it! YEAH, we made it to Utah!

Logan, Utah is just east of Salt Lake City. It was another long day in the car with lots of frustration. I was very relieved to arrive here.

Finding a motel to stay in was frustrating once we got to Logan. I had not pre-booked. And the first motel we stopped at was $139 per night.

The motel we ended up in was clean and was under $80 for the night.

We went for a walk in the evening.

We came to a park and there was a yoga class going on. OH YES! Let's do it!

AHHHHH...

I told George that tomorrow we are going to bike a bit before we drive some more. It has been too many days in a row of long times in the car.

Let's do what we can to keep our sanity and bodies healthy. Tomorrow we ride before we ride.

Yay! On **Day 49** we got to ride our trikes a little bit! The city of Logan, Utah sits in a flat area surrounded by hills. It has some trails.

The streets are VERY wide here. There is room for two lanes, parking on both sides, and more. Yet there is hardly any traffic on the back streets. We learned later the wide streets are for cattle drives and combines.

We got on a trail and it quickly turned to gravel and started up a hill.

It got so steep our back wheels started slipping on the gravel. I got up the hill by getting off and pushing my trike. I told George to stay put and I would come back to push him up the hill.

I got to the top and locked my brakes and looked back, George was trying to get out of his trike. He has lost the ability to get off his trike on a hill and kept falling back into the seat.

"STAY SEATED," I yelled. "I am coming to push."

I pushed, it was tough, and I wrenched my back a bit.

239

At a park there was information about the irrigation canals. The first farmers to irrigate used workers and when they couldn't pay them, they paid them with land and water rights.

Canal 7 in 1947. Courtesy Utah State Historical Society.

In the van we continued our journey toward Colorado.

We began seeing lots of billboards for Little America. It seemed like the Wall Drug in South Dakota. The advertising worked on us. We took a break!

The place was humming with travelers, out in the middle of nowhere. So far out in fact that there was housing behind the store for the employees.

In the store, I told George I saw some earrings I like. He was anxious to buy them for me. Sweet.

FINALLY, we are getting close to Rock Springs, WY.

Much of the mining in the area is for soda ash. Used in soap and toothpaste and all kinds of things.

In Rock Springs we found the Eco-Lodge with a senior rate of $65.

241

Day 50 - Miles Of "Butts"

I know that probably many of the millions of travelers through this area over the past few centuries have entertained themselves by pronouncing buttes as butts. We are not above this base humor.

Unfortunately we passed up the opportunity to see the Pilot Butte. I am sure it was amazing.

The breakfast at the motel we grabbed some extra toast for lunch. On this trip our previous efforts to cut down on bread have gone out the window in exchange for convenience.

I think that a few elderly people live in the motel. I have heard that some elderly have found it less costly than assisted living apartments and the morning meal is included. There are coffee and cookies available all day and the desk attendant is available 24/7 to open jars for you.

George seemed good this morning. He talked a tiny bit more and his voice was his old strong voice. He did most the packing, and he seemed to be doing well at it. I thanked him.

I let the iPad take us where it may. I picked the shortest route. We were heading to our next Affordable Travel Club host near Steamboat Springs, Colorado.

As soon as we left Rock Springs, the countryside opened up. I said, "WOW! They could shoot westerns here. There are no telephone wires, no roads other than this one, no cars, no planes, not even jet streams!"

For miles and miles and miles...

And lots of buttes to look at..."So many beautiful butts," I say, and we both laugh.

About 40 miles out, the road turned to gravel.

It was a decently maintained road and we were able to go about 40 mph.

They were working to conserve the natural resources.

Another historical stop had a path to a rock with ancient drawings. 100 to 400 AD they were dated... impressive.

For lunch we still had some of the lavender-infused jam we bought at the Portland Farmers Market.

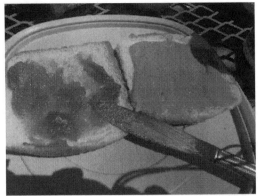

We learned at a kiosk there that Butch Cassidy and a few other notorious thieves liked hanging out in the area. The sheep/cattleman wars occurred over use of the land here.

Further down the road we learned that the highway we were traveling on, Hwy 40, was completed in 1920 and ran coast to coast.

We entered Colorado. YEAH!!!!

We stopped at an outcropping and saw that these rocks had faces. One looks like an alien and the other looks like a mouse or ???

This was a good spot to do our exercises, under the watchful eye of some beautiful horses.

Our hosts live outside of Oak Creek, an old mining town.

246

We were 7,000 feet above sea level. George and I were feeling the dryness and the altitude. I was feeling a bit sick, as if I had taken a vitamin on an empty stomach.

We arrived at Debbie and Mike's home way up in the hills on a gravel road.

Mike gave us a map of Steamboat Springs where we could ride a bike trail in town.

Debbie served me wine and I even drank a diet coke trying to calm my stomach. It worked. BUT I STILL FEEL THIRSTY! She said we need to drink five times as much water as we normally drink because it is so dry.

We had brought Subway sandwiches and we dined on their deck.

Then I drove with George down to a lake to walk on a trail.

When we got back to the parking lot, George had to use the restroom. While he was in there I took some pictures. It was still very windy.

He took a while, that made me a bit nervous. I was about to knock and ask if he was okay, when he emerged.

We get back and Mike offers to watch a MAD MAX movie with George! They watch that while I upload pictures and take a shower.

When I am done with my shower, George is done with the movie and undressing in the bedroom. He starts picking dried poop off his hairy bottom and putting it in his other hand. I guide him into the bathroom. (FORTUNATELY we have the whole lower level to ourselves because he is walking naked through the common area.) I tell him to take a shower.

He can't figure out how to start the shower (a standard lever). So I start the shower and tell him how to get in and tell him to wash his butt good.

I then rinse out his crusty underwear and fight back tears. I wonder if we can keep using Affordable Travel Club and Evergreen Club when things like this are happening.

George didn't seem embarrassed. When he climbed into bed I hugged him and he said, "I love you," like he always does.

This is "Sundowning"

A person with dementia can do well for part of the day and then more symptoms appear as the day goes on.

Sometimes caregivers will complain that they are dealing with this dementia and that the children or the friends or the neighbors don't see the dementia symptoms. "They have no clue what it is like!"

Outsiders may only see the times when the person with dementia is doing well. They can act normal during a visit to the doctor.

If you are suspicious that a family member or friend is having dementia symptoms, arrange to spend a full long day (or several) with them. Be sure to be with them into the evening.

Living with reduced brain capacity is tiring. At the end of the day the person with dementia runs out of steam and makes more mistakes. They may become more anxious or angry or afraid.

George was able to walk and talk well during the day. He did not wet his pants. He appreciated the beauty of where we were. He laughed at the jokes. It wasn't until later in the day he was picking poop off his butt hair and not knowing what to do about it.

Some people with dementia are more apt to pace and wander in the evening. They may get violent, yell, rock in their chairs and groan. They may hallucinate.

Can you imagine how scary it is to have thoughts and visions you can't trust? Sometimes everything and everyone they look at is unfamiliar at first and it takes a while to figure it out.

I am once again grateful we are able to do this trip now.

Day 51 – Incompetent Travel Agent

I didn't write it all down! Oh my. Thank goodness George's critical brain isn't working. And my brother was forgiving too.

I started the day out grumpy. Insomnia kept me awake for most the night. At 2:00 a.m. I looked out the open window of our bedroom. I enjoyed a cool breeze filled with the fragrance of pine. The night sky was not hindered by city lights allowing me to see the lights of millions of stars.

I went back to bed and finally slept. George woke before me and got up and got dressed. I tried to lie in bed and get a bit more sleep.

"Don't start to pack yet," I tell him.

He sits on the edge of the bed with his iPad.

"Go out into the other room, please," I said. (We had the whole lower level of Mike and Debbie's home to use.) George grumbled back at me like he used to do when he thought I was being too bossy.

"Do you need me to log you in first?" I asked.

"No," he said and went to sit in the living room.

In a couple minutes he came back in and sat on the edge of the bed.

"You need me to log you in?" I asked.

"No," he said.

"Are you sure?" I ask. He hands me his iPad.

"Log me in," he says.

I log him into the internet and then he sits down on the bed again. I send him into the living room.

He only lasts what seems like five minutes. I am resentful. I get out of bed and get ready for the day.

After some coffee I feel much better.

Mike engaged George in conversation about George's days in the navy. I sometimes stepped in to elaborate or translate George's few words. He speaks too fast, jumbles and stutters. Mike and Debbie were very kind.

We had breakfast on the deck while three humming birds competed over our heads.

After breakfast, we said our goodbyes. Debbie said to me, "I think what you are doing, traveling with George, is wonderful. I really admire what you are doing."

I thanked her. I know this is what we must do. And it gives me time to enjoy the parts of George that are coming out as the left side of his brain fades.

For example the day before we were driving a long distance through the Wyoming desert and I broke out into song. "Home, Home on the Range... where the deer and the antelope play..." And George laughed and joined in singing with me!

OH MY! Forty years we have been together. Forty years of him not liking my singing. I think the only time he sang with me was in church or the Happy Birthday song, and maybe the national anthem at an event.

I was thrilled.

I drove us to Steamboat Springs, a ski town only about twenty-seven miles away, where we were going to go on a short trike ride before heading to meet up with my brother.

When we got out of the car, I smelled sulfur. Then I saw we had parked next to a spring. Steamboat Springs has several hot springs. The plaque by this spring said it was 72 degrees. It was bubbling but not boiling hot. The bubbles were sulfur gas.

One of my front tires was flat. George changed the tire and tube. We will have to find a bike shop that handles trikes in Boulder/Denver area to replace our spares. Not all bike shops carry the small twenty-inch tires and tubes our trikes need.

The bike trail in Steamboat runs along the river through town. It is only about six miles long.

On our ride I started noticing that most everyone was slim and fit... even the children. I think the whole time in the city I only saw a few overweight people.

Back in the van we stopped at the chamber to double check our route since my iPad didn't work and I don't like depending on the car's GPS. We took Route 40 toward Granby, Colorado.

I pulled off a couple times to get pictures of the beautiful scenery.

We were meeting up with my brother, Larry, in Grand Lake, Colorado. Larry was driving up from Arizona.

We turned a corner and the landscape changed dramatically. Part of the Colorado River had cut through these hills.

I got a text from my brother. He was in Granby. "What next," he asked.

It turned out I didn't have a full address for where we were staying and the car navigator could not find it with the information I had.

We met Larry in Granby and headed for Grand Lake. I felt SOOO incompetent.

Neither of us had internet access through our devices so I could not look up the full address. I had no phone number for the owner of where were staying. I had booked it through Vacation Rental By Owner (VRBO). I had looked up the place on Google maps before we left Florida. I thought I knew where it was and how to get there. I was over confident.

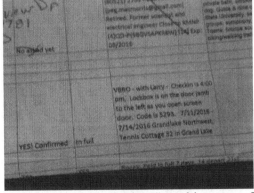

In Larry's notes he had "Soda Springs" on his notes. I didn't know what that was. We ended up driving into Grand Lakes and asking at a Real Estate office that fortunately was still open at 5:00 p.m.

He said the only "Tennis" address he knew of was in Soda Springs, about four miles away.

Once we got to the Soda Springs neighborhood we had to drive around and around looking for Tennis 32.

I was so relieved to find it!

We unpacked and then Larry drove us back to downtown Grand Lake for dinner. After dinner we strolled up and down the main drag. One store had a nest of birds over their porch light.

George and Larry watched a movie... Twister. I worked on email and this blog. The internet was very slow. I left the pictures to upload overnight.

Tomorrow we go explore Rocky Mountain National Park.

Day 52 – 53 - Rocky Mountain National

On **day 52**, when I got up, Larry was already awake and had coffee made. We didn't have any milk. George ate Raisin Bran without it.

Years ago George would have had to go to the store to get some. Before dementia he knew what he wanted and he couldn't flex. Now he just goes with it and doesn't complain. This change is something I am grateful for.

We all piled into Larry's car for our trip into Rocky Mountain National Park

At the first intersection, Larry sneezed his signature sneeze. Instead of "Ah CHEW" he said, "Aww SHIT".

George and I laughed and I said "Bless you."

Larry said, "Thankuverymuch" like Elvis Presley

There was one place in the park that Larry wanted to see. It was a big meadow where they have a camera set up, and he has been checking in on the webcam.

We were surprised to see almost all the taller trees are dead. The hills are grey with dead trees.

The first visitors' station was having a program on flowers with a little hike.

The ranger explained the different parts of the flower.

The ranger told us to walk up the trail and count the number of different flowers we find.

I got caught up on taking pictures of the flowers instead. I counted 17 different kinds of flowers.

It was glorious, looking down at the flowers and grasses and then looking up at the magnificent surroundings.

SOOO many dead trees, I asked the ranger about it.

He said it is a beetle native to the US. I learned later that the only thing that stops it is a deep freeze (harsh winter) or a fire. The damage is from Canada to Mexico. The beetle goes under the bark and lays its eggs; the larva destroy the tree.

The younger trees are resistant. Once the beetle has gotten all the older trees it is done. The forest comes back. The beetle returns about every fifteen to twenty years.

We learned that a dandelion is not one flower. We learned that flies do a lot of the pollinating.

The ranger gave us magnifying glasses to see the flowers up close.

We left the flower lecture before it was done. TOO MUCH INFORMATION for our brains.

Then off to a waterfall hike. We chose a short hike.

In the thin air, the uphill climb still had us all panting within a short time. There were a lot of tourists there. The park gets 2 million guests a year.

We went back to our cabin to rest a bit.

Later, George and I went to get ingredients for root beer floats. A moose was lying next to the road across from the store. We trotted across the street and got a quick picture.

YEAH!!! ROOTBEER FLOATS!

Then we went back to the park for a sunset hike in hopes of seeing some wildlife.

We didn't see any. George and I stood and watched a black spot way out in the field. Was it moving? Was it getting bigger? It remained a black spot.

Tomorrow I want to use the library internet. There is a band supposed to play on the town square at 5:00 p.m.

Rocky Mountain Music

"We will do that tomorrow morning then," George says.

I searched through my recent memory. We had been silent, was there anything I had mentioned about tomorrow? I had mentioned using the fitness room at the community center. Was that it? I had told him we were going to take the back roads to Carbondale, Colorado. Was that it?

"What will we do tomorrow morning?" I ask George.

"Have sex," he says.

I look at him, he hadn't said a thing during our whole walk other than to echo what I had said or agree with something I had said.

We were getting close to our cabin and the end of our walk. Maybe he came along on the walk because he had expectations?

"Did you think we were going to have sex on this walk?" I ask.

"No," he shakes his head and grins.

I am puzzled. This just came out of the blue, like he had been having a conversation in his head and thought I was listening in. I shrug askance. He mirrors my action.

"Are you just giving me a warning?" I ask.

"Yes," he nods and he smiles at me.

"Ok then! Thanks for the advance notice!"

That conversation occurred at the end of this day, our last day in the condo near Rocky Mountain National Park with my brother. At the beginning of the day I got a few moments to myself before George got out of bed. I went for a brisk walk.

George walks a slower pace and I usually am several paces ahead of him. If I walk next to him he walks slower yet to get behind me.

Besides all the extra eating on this trip, the long bike rides aren't as frequent, the yoga sessions less frequent, the weight-lifting has been hardly at all.

It was cold and there was a breeze that cut right through both my light jackets. The walk was short, I returned to our condo.

George was already up. Larry wanted to buy us breakfast and then we all wanted to explore the park some more. I packed a lunch and we all got in Larry's car and he drove us to downtown Grand Lake.

We hoped that entering the park while the air was still cool and the shadows were long that we might see some wildlife.

Back in the car we began the climb to the continental divide.

Larry compiles CD's of music. He had put together a CD with music from different times of his life to be played at his funeral. It was

enjoyable listening to it. He said he had sent a copy to his son and wants to write up a couple pages explaining the significance of each song.

Who would think that preparing for one's own funeral could be such fun!

When the song "How much is that doggie in the window" came on, I heard George singing along in the back seat! Wow! He is happy and that is a very good thing.

We continued to climb. Near the top is the Alpine Visitors Center.

We entered one building, and I used the restroom and asked George if he needed to use the restroom.

"No," he said.

Not five minutes later we entered another building, and George asked where the restrooms are. I took him back to the first building and the restrooms.

Larry bought a National Park Monopoly game, not to play, but he liked the ranger hat playing piece.

The construction and maintenance of the roads through the mountains is something that is awe-inspiring. We look at the stone walls that sit on very steep inclines and wonder how they ever did it and do it still.

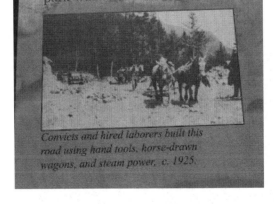

Convicts and hired laborers built this road using hand tools, horse-drawn wagons, and steam power, c. 1925.

I want to ascend the steps to the top of the mountain. George wants to go too. There are no railings. I am a bit concerned. We start to climb. I notice a building with tall sticks on it. Later I learned the poles are to find the building when it gets completely covered in snow.

We bundled up with two jackets. The wind was cold and got stronger as we climbed.

I counted steps but lost count around 130.

At the top was a kiosk talking about the plants and animals that survive in this cold altitude. There is a bird with feathers on its feet and eye-lids. The yellow-bellied Marmot hibernates seven to eight months of the year.

I was surprised at the beauty and variety of flowers in this area where trees cannot grow. The plant below is a kind of alpine "Chicks and Hens".

We started the decent. I stopped every once in a while to look back and check on George. "I'm fine," he'd say.

Back at the parking lot we looked back up the mountain. So many beautiful flowers!

We made our way back down the mountain.

Larry kindly pulled over when I sighed over the beauty of the flowers along a rock wall. I got out and took some pictures.

Back near the entrance of the park we had our picnic lunch of PB&J and fruit.

We went to the Grand Lakes library.

George looked at magazines (I had to help him find some. He used to love reading about the study of genetics and Time magazine had an article on the topic.) He still enjoys automobile magazines.

The internet was fast at the library, and I was able to upload pictures and write. After an hour George started coming over every few minutes. He would lightly scratch my back and say, "How ya doin'?"

I was relieved to get all caught up.

At 5:00 p.m. there was music on the square in front of the library. The band was quite good.

Larry wanted a CD. So he sent me up to get one. Then he came and helped me pick one out. Without prompting, George took our picture while we were hunting through the choices.

After supper I said I was going for a walk and George said, "I'll go with you."

We walked around the neighborhood, George not saying anything except to agree or echo something I said. We walked until the mosquitoes drove us to turn around, and that is when I got the "warning" from George. *"We'll do it tomorrow morning then."*

Sex and the Demented

People caring for their parents have a whole different mental and emotional hump to get over. For me as a spouse of a husband who is sexually competent, this is a big issue for me. Not because I desire sex, but because he does. He has become like a child in many ways. Yet, even as his abilities and personality diminish, he still wants us to act like we always have as husband and wife.

I have heard from others that men with dementia can stay interested until the day they die. The ability and interest survives long after many other abilities end.

I (and probably many wives and husbands that are dementia caregivers) struggle with when (if ever) to stop agreeing to sex. When is the time to draw the line? This is probably a question that individuals need to answer for themselves. I am guessing there is not a moral text on the issue. No one else can provide that guideline.

Day 54 - Longest Trip Ever

July 14, 2016, we had said our "goodbyes" to Larry the night before. He said he was going to get an early start and would probably be gone already when we woke up.

When I got up George was still sleeping, and Larry was gone.

One thing not much affected by George's brain deterioration is his memory. Let's just say, he remembered his one agenda item for the day.

Today is our fifty-fourth day of the trip! Our bike trip from Illinois to Florida on our tricycles took us fifty-three days. Today we are now officially on our "longest trip ever".

For breakfast we had Raisin Bran and ice cream. Now before you gasp, just let me remind you... what is ice cream? ... Cream and sugar.

Which reminds me; I also put a scoop of the stuff in my coffee before I tossed the rest of the ice cream in the trash.

We went into the clubhouse to exercise. It felt so good to work out again. I told George that I was joining the gym again when we got home. We had quit when we retired and didn't think we had it in the budget. "I would rather picnic more often on our bike rides and still work out," I said. George agreed.

I am nervous about him working out. His body awareness isn't what it used to be. He is lifting with a round back at times which is a no-no.

Today we were headed to Carbondale, Colorado where we will stay for a whole week. It is a room in someone's home I booked through Airbnb.

A ranger at the Forest Service office said the back road I wanted to take was open and in good shape. So off we went on another adventure!

First we were to take Hwy 40.

The next town just seemed unexpected; I hadn't yet encountered the town on the map where I had planned to turn off Hwy 40.

I pulled over and studied the map. DANG! I had turned the wrong way out of the Forest Service Office! I was now 30 miles in the wrong direction!

Do I go back or just head for Interstate 70? I do like I always do when faced with a dilemma. I ask George. "Keep going this direction," he said.

So we did. Up over the mountain to get to Interstate 70 and then up over the mountains again.

George took the picture below when we went through a tunnel.

We pulled off in a town to get some groceries. The town was full of roundabouts. I asked the grocery clerk where we could go to eat our picnic lunch.

Go to the Welcome Center, three roundabouts down, she told us.

Yay! We got a table in the shade right by a roaring river. Smiles.

The Airbnb hostess sent me several texts letting me know she would be home late and giving instructions for how to get in and which room was ours.

We are to take our shoes off at the door. We put everything we thought we needed outside the door before entering.

Our hostess has a lot of boots!

We relaxed a while, and then we walk to downtown.

We passed the theater in town and I saw that a movie was playing. I told George, we should go tonight! He chuckled.

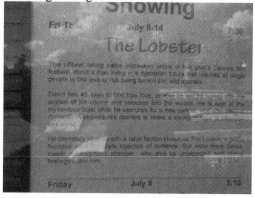

We stopped in the library to see what posters and events they might have the week we are here.

Then we walked back to our home for the whole week.

We have the lower level to ourselves. The back deck has a ski-lift chair to swing on.

Rosie gave us the name for restaurants where we could get breakfast in the morning. Later we went to the movie... THE LOBSTER.

UGH! It was AWFUL. Not as bad as a poke in the eye with a sharp stick, but as bad as watching someone deliberately poke themselves in the eye with a sharp stick. (Yes, that was a scene in this movie.)

When we got back from our movie, I didn't know what the Airbnb etiquette was. Should we go upstairs and chat for a while. I stood on the landing and Rosie came to speak with us.

Rosie has a business in Aspen, teaching Pilates and offering massage. Tomorrow we ride!

Day 55 - Rio Grande Trail

Yeah! We get to ride the Rio Grande Trail to Aspen, Colorado today. I am excited.

We bike to breakfast.

We were maybe two miles from home, and George already needed the bathroom when we arrived. There is no bathroom at this outdoor trailer kind of food kiosk.

The owner told us a block down was the city building with restrooms. I was worried that George would get lost. Directional impairment was one of the first noticeable dementia symptoms I had observed in George. After I watched him go down the road and turn out of sight, I told the owner I would be right back and I dashed off after George and helped him find his way.

We had two sandwiches, two coffees, $20.

The trail crosses Main Street near downtown Carbondale. Soon we were on the very gradual incline toward the ski town of Aspen, Colorado.

We came to a detour sign. "Cougar activity" was the reason.

It put us on a road without a shoulder that was kind of busy at times.

The detour was well marked. We have been on bike detours before that were not marked at all. So thank you, Colorado!

We were averaging a little over seven miles per hour. It was going to be a long climb to Aspen.

Thirty-two miles and we made it to Aspen.
We parked our bikes right by this life-like statue.

I handed George the camera.

We found Victoria's, one block away for a light lunch.

Victoria's is across the street from a huge bike and bus center in downtown Aspen. Great going, Aspen!

The ride back was fast! We were going 12-20 mph most of the time.

If you ride the Rio Grande Trail, just know there are NO FACILITIES. Take lots of water and prepare to make do. I kept asking George if he had to go.

"No," he said. And there were no accidents...

Back on the trail after the detour, I saw this snake on the trail, digesting a meal.

A little further down on the trail I saw two smaller snakes curled on the trail. I stopped and got off my trike to walk back to take a picture.

I returned to the trikes and went to get on my trike. Right next to my trike were two more snakes.

They slithered off before I got the camera ready.

Back in town we stopped at City Market for stuff for supper. We got sweet potatoes, cauliflower and salad stuff.

I pulled out and rode down the street a couple blocks before I checked my rear-view mirror for George. NOT THERE!

I go back to the parking lot. NOT THERE! I ask several people just entering the store if she had seen him. Nope!

I don't know what to do. Panic!

I start biking in another direction, and there he is on the other side of the street. He is heading back toward the store and looking around, but he doesn't see me. I yell for him until he sees me. I give him directions to follow me on his side of the street until we reach a cross walk where it is safe to cross.

We get home after 64 miles. Not bad for a 68-year old guy with dementia! High fives!

Day 56 - Bells is full of Smells

Remember back in Wisconsin that my friend Kathi whose husband is also going through dementia advised me to always pack a bag with:
1) Wet wipes;
2) Change of clothes for your loved one; and
3) Large plastic bag (to put the soiled stuff in).

I listened a little bit. I put wet wipes in the backpack today.

I saw there was a guided hike at 10:15 today at "Maroon Bells." I didn't know what "Maroon Bells" was but I remember one of the last things our Airbnb host had said before she left us on our own for the weekend was: "Have you been to Maroon Bells?" and "You've got to go."

I didn't remember what she said, but then this hike came up in my internet search. I also learned in the "How to get there" section that the public transport takes people from Carbondale to Aspen and to Maroon Bells.

I packed the backpack with wet-wipes, jackets, water, granola bars, nuts, an apple, compass, phone, and camera. I drove to the park-and-ride to catch the bus.

I didn't know which bus to take; I asked the drivers before we got on. The bus charts posted were like reading Greek to me.

The first bus that arrived had a helpful driver. He explained the next bus was the one we should get on. It would go all the way to Aspen with 20 stops in between. One of the stops was where we were to get off for Maroon Bells.

Seniors over 65 ride free. We are seniors!

The bus began to fill up more at each stop. It was pretty full by the time we got off.

The driver told us when to get off. We get off as told, but then we didn't know what to do. Where do we go now? This was Maroon Castle stop. Where were the bells? We were supposed to catch the hike at the "Info Center". Do we go to the castle? Is that the Info Center? A digital sign said catch the bus to Maroon Bells.... Which bus? Where?

Fortunately another bus came and dropped off a couple who had been given instructions by their motel concierge. Catch the bus to Maroon Bells here. We were still confused when a bus pulled up. He was going to Maroon Bells.

The bus took us to a huge ski resort area. Signs said to buy bus tickets to Maroon Bells there. We went inside, and I bought two senior tickets to Maroon Bells. $6 each.

A LOT of other people had the same idea. The bus to Maroon Bells was full.

The bus driver explained that in the 1800's this was mining territory. Then the Silver Act devalued silver, and Aspen as a town went down to about 200 people, mostly farming and ranching. Then some guy started a ski resort in the 1940's. Now it booms with tourism.

So many people were driving up and walking around the Maroon Bells Wilderness Area that they were destroying the vegetation and air. So the area ruled that all people must come up by bus.

I saw cars up there, though. I learned that cars are allowed past the gate before 8:00 a.m. and after 5:00 p.m.

The bus stopped at a place with cave-like structures for waiting for the bus and for restrooms.

We arrived 15 minutes after the guided hike was to start. I asked the ranger if they had left yet. "Yes, but if you hurry down to the lake, you can probably hook up with them."

Hurrying with George is not really hurrying. With his dementia he walks slower, and breaking into a trot doesn't even happen if we are crossing a busy road.

It was earlier in the day and if I moved faster, he would pick up the pace a bit.

Wow, the view was awesome. I told George, "Wow, I can't believe we are here. This is surreal."

George said, "It is, I was thinking the same thing."

I thought, that is a lot for him to say. He is doing well this morning.

There is a nice paved sidewalk to the lake. There were lots of groups of people down there. Which one was the guided hike?

I hovered near each group as we passed. I thought, if someone looks or sounds like a ranger, I will ask.

At the far end of the lake I heard a young guy talking with a group of four about the Beaver Dam. He had a name-tag on! "Is this the 10:15 hike?" I asked.

They asked if we were here to do the lower lake or the Crater Lake hike. It takes one and a half hours to get to Crater Lake they tell me..

We will do the Crater Lake hike. George was standing erect. He was sharp. We can do this, I thought. One of the guides led us to a trail and went with us, just George and I.

The guide was just out of college with a degree in Environmental Biology. He is working for a non-profit that does environmental education. He said he is happy to be out hiking and getting paid for it.

The most interesting thing we learned was about aspen trees. In an avalanche an aspen can bend to the ground and recover when the snow melts. Its outer bark is thin and an inner skin has chloroform in it to produce energy for the plant like the leaves.

The aspen self-trims its lower limbs since they don't get much light anyway.

And if you rub your hand on the bark you come up with a powder which is a sunscreen of about SPF 5.

Aspen multiply with seeds like a normal plant, but they also spread through the root system making a clone in such a way that the host (first) tree doesn't have to compete for resources (sun and soil) with the second tree.

On the far side of the mountain is one of the largest aspen ... clusters (clone bunch or group of genetically identical aspen) in the United States.

Up up up we climb over rocky terrain. I keep checking on George, "How are you doing?"

"I'm fine," he says.

I hear no stumbling. I keep thinking we are almost there. We rest and keep going.

The guide, (Josh is his name), shows us where the snow collects in crevices high up and then either a powder snow falls on top of ice or melt underneath allows the snow to slide down the mountain in an avalanche carrying rock with it.

At one avalanche area, the rock had piled up at the bottom creating a shoot or ski-jump effect. So when the snow comes down in an avalanche it shoots across the valley and over the trail where we were standing.

Look at the terrain we were hiking over. There were a LOT of people on the trail. I would suspect that this park also gets two million people a year. There were so many people hiking. We often had to stop and pull over and let hikers pass.

And there were a LOT of hikers with over-night packs. There were groups of two to four going up or coming back. Some hikers had bedrolls and pots hanging from their packs.

We started to descend toward the lake. It was warm still, but the wind picked up, blowing the fine dust created by thousands and thousands of feet.

Josh quickly took our picture by the "Maroon Bells" at Crater Lake. Then he said goodbye and off he went.

I was glad he didn't stick around. I knew he was anxious to walk faster than we were going. Also, I wanted to rest and eat our snack and enjoy the view for a while. Plus, I had to go to the bathroom. There were no facilities. And there were so many people! I worried that George might have to go to. But I asked if he had to go potty and he said, "No."

One end of the lake was full of logs. Josh said there was no outlet, there. It was the prevailing winds that drove the logs to this end of the lake.

We sat on a log and ate our snacks and that was when I started to smell it. A faint whiff of pooh...

I didn't ask George. I thought it could be my coffee breath... I hoped it was my breath...

We began the long hike back. It is mostly downhill. I looked back at George. He was leaning back.

"Are you OK?" I ask.

"I'm fine," he smiles his dopey dementia smile that tells me he is getting foggy in thought as well as unstable on his feet.

We rest more often. We stretch. We do some of our exercises. Nothing seems to help for longer than a few minutes.

At one point I look back, and he is weaving like a drunk. We rest again. I take a picture of him leaning back and show it to him. I am hoping that if he corrects his stance, he won't be so wobbly.

We rest. I smell the pooh. I check my breath. I ask George, "Did you poop your pants?"

"Ya," he smiles.

There were many people passing us. At least there will be help if we need it, I thought.

We run out of water. A woman offers us hers. We take it. She is on her way to the Crater. I feel bad, but she insists. I give it all to George. We are making progress moving from sitting place to sitting place.

We watch younger folks moving quickly over the rocky trail. George says, "Ahhh, to be young again."

"I know, I have been thinking about that a lot on this trip," I say. He says he has been too.

When we were young and able, we were working all the time. Rarely did we get a chance to travel and explore. Certainly not for 56 days.

At one point a ranger passes. "Are you OK?" she asks.

"I'm fine," says George.

"He is dizzy," I say and she says to drink a lot and take our time. She said that there are a lot of people on the trail so just tell them if we need help.

Finally I can see the lake where we started this hike. HURRAY! But we are moving so very very VERY slow!

People are gathered, all trying to get pictures of a huge moose. By the time I get there he is lying in the grass. People keep trying to get closer to take a better picture. I hear a ranger say that the moose already charged a woman trying to get a closer picture. The woman was surprised the moose charged her.

The ranger said, "She could have been killed. We are predators of the moose; of course he is going to protect his space."

In the late 1980s and early 1990s I was active trying to educate people about population growth and its impact on the natural resources. It is hard to believe that the world population then had not yet reached six billion. Now it is over seven billion and growing still. And when my mother was born it was around two billion. That is a LOT of growth.

I am thinking we shouldn't go to National Parks anymore. We shouldn't be adding our footsteps and pictures to the millions of others who have gone and will go on the same trails and roads as us. I have thoughts of just going home now.

We get back on the sidewalk and I take George's hand. He is still very wobbly and very, very VERY slow. I start dreaming of a family style bathroom where I can go in and help him get cleaned up. There I can rinse out his pants. He is foggy. He will need help.

The Maroon Bells look bigger from here. Still awesome. As people pass, I wonder if they smell the pooh.

We arrive at the restrooms. Pit Toilets... men and women designation.... No family bathroom.

I hand George the wet wipes and separate a few so he doesn't use all of them in one wipe. I explain it is a pit toilet so he can throw them down the toilet. I send him in. I worry. I wait...

I go use the women's toilet and notice there is another exit door on the other side of the cave/building. Oh oh...

I sit on the floor by the entrance to the men's, and I worry that he might go out the other door and wander around looking for me.

I make some noise so he can hear me.

There is a drinking fountain, thank goodness! I fill our thermoses.

I wait and wait. I wonder if I should yell for him. He finally emerges, smiling. He hands me the bag that the wet wipes were in. There is one or two left.

"Did you wipe out your underwear good?" I ask.

"They are in my pocket," he said.

I have him take them out and put them in the plastic bag with the wipes. Now there is pooh on his pocket. Oh well....

There is a drinking fountain. I run the water and have him rinse off his hands.

There are a lot of people waiting for the bus. I am so tired. Fortunately there is room for both of us to sit.

I think, "Now we are those old people for whom young and able folks are supposed to give up their seats."

The bus is packed. Fortunately, again we have a seat. There are a lot of people standing.

At the ski resort we ask where we can catch a bus to get back to Carbondale. We have to catch a bus to Aspen and then get on the bus to Carbondale.

I had thought we would dine in Aspen, explore more of downtown Aspen. But now George had a wet spot on the front of his pants, and I can still smell pooh and we are tired.

On the bus I close my eyes for quite a while.

George touches my arm, "Have I told you yet today how much I love you?" he asks.

"I love you too," I say. And I think to myself, is he still my George? How much of George is still there?

I want to get some wine or beer. I remember learning that sometimes caregivers become alcoholics. It is tempting to dull the grief or feel a reward for this constant care. I could see myself turning to food too. Let me see... marijuana is legal in Colorado for recreational use....

I am thinking I should stop at the grocery store, but I still smell pooh and I know that George won't stay in the car. He will want to walk through the store with me.

No problem, there is always PB&J at home

Fortunately our host is still out of town, we have the place to ourselves. I send George into the shower and I rinse out his underwear... having to swish it in the toilet like I used to do with baby diapers over forty years ago.

We have lived a long time! I am feeling sad that we are at this stage of it. I think of a neighbor who was a caretaker for her husband for 27 years! He had a stroke at an earlier age.

I remember the last year of his life she lost patience. She was angry that he no longer followed directions. He would grin at her as if defying her directions like a naughty child of two.

Will I be able to ask friends for help? They offer their support, but when it comes right down to spending a few hours with George so I can go work out or do something several times a week... will they be able to help? Will I be able to afford to pay someone to help?

It is times like this, when I am reminded of what is ahead that I worry... and feel tired.

I think if it weren't for our house and cat-sit commitment later this month, I might just start our journey home. I am so tired....

I pick out clean clothes for George. He is walking better but is still pretty foggy.

I realize this was all my fault. I should not take George on long walks in the woods anymore.

After supper we go to a laundromat. It is only three blocks away. $3 for a wash.

While we wait for the clothes to wash and dry, we read our books.

I pull the clothes out of the dryer. His underwear still smells like pooh. I put them back in the dirty clothes bag.

George helps me fold clothes. I make a stack for him to carry to the car.

I hunt out a gas station and get us a couple drumstick ice cream treats. Comfort food....

I am grateful that George can still read and stream programs on his iPad. That gives me a moment to upload pictures, keep a record of our experiences, and plan our activities.

I have some friends going through this whose husbands are not as cooperative and pleasant as George.

From now on I hope I remember to pack a full supply of wet-wipes, and a change of pants.

Tomorrow is Sunday. The bike trail will be busy. I don't know what we will do. At this point, I would like to just rest.

Days 57 - 60 Carbondale Moments

Today I spent the whole morning writing the last three days of travel diaries, responding to emails, and just getting some things done. Then it was 12:30 already!!! I moved my computer from the kitchen to the bedroom where we are keeping our stuff.

George had occupied himself with reading and Sudoku on his iPad during the morning. But he was starting to hover. He was hungry. I mentioned going to a restaurant. He went out and stood next to the car.

I thought we would try one of the restaurants that our hostess, Rosie, had recommended -- Dos Gringos. I gathered some things up for the afternoon. Then I remembered that Rosie would be arriving back from her weekend away. I needed to get our stuff out of the common areas and clean up the kitchen. All while I was doing this, George stood by the car waiting.

Water bottles filled, camera, iPad, purse, sweat shirts, nuts, a baggie with wet-wipes. I didn't know what our plans were after lunch, but I wanted to be ready in case we decided to ride or walk or just hang out someplace.

We both liked Dos Gringos. The burritos we had were full of black beans, seasoned tofu, fried sweet peppers and onions, brown rice, spring greens, and salsa. Yeah for delicious vegetarian food!

We decided to pull the bikes out of the car and go exploring.

First we pedaled into town. I was going to zig zag the streets for a while. Sometimes we come upon surprises that delight us. Like a large, welded and painted bright-pink bunny in someone's front yard. And across the street someone had glued a little plastic toy rhino to their mailbox. This neighborhood has a little fun.

"Want to ride 12 miles to Glenwood?" I ask George. "Or do you want to keep zig zagging."

"Ride 12 miles," he says.

We rode the Rio Grande Trail to Glenwood Springs.

We stopped and I refilled our waters at a McDonalds. It was dry and warm, and in 12 miles we had consumed all our water.

Back on the trail we passed this fence made of old skis.

I wanted to keep this ride a bit shorter since we had overdone our hike yesterday. Riding back it only took us eight miles to use up all our water again. There was a gas station and liquor store across the highway. I got a bottle of water for right away and a bottle of something else for later.

When our ride was over we put our bikes in the car and we went back into DOS GRINGOS for supper.

When we walked in, half of the restaurant seating area was used up by a circle of people in chairs playing stringed instruments. They were playing old country/cowboy and gospel music. "May the circle... be unbroken... by and by Lord..." SMILES!

It was already 7:00 when we arrived back "home." We sat out on the back lower deck and read. I drank my bottle and we shared some cookies we had bought. THEY WERE GOOD!

I finished my book. At one point a surprise twist in the story had me go "OH MY!" out loud.

George wanted to know what happened. "You have to read this book, it is soooo good!" <u>Big Little Lies</u> by L. Moriarty.

Our hostess came home and we invited her to come down and join us, but she had lots to do before she went back to work tomorrow.

One of the things she had to do was water her plants on the upper deck ... which leaked through and dripped on us. Whoops!

We both moved into the spare room. I finished my book.

It was a good finish to a good day.

It is **Day 58** and I am missing social interaction. I search again for local events here and tried to reach out via Facebook and Twitter to find some bike group and social group to connect with in Boulder. I joined some Meetup groups but discover they don't have any gatherings planned.

Later in the morning I drove us through a carwash. I took a picture because this was a moment of delight. The carwash had lights on the suds that went from blue to green to pink. I took several pictures, but my timing was off and every picture had pink suds.

We giggled when it was our turn to get slathered in colorful suds.

Next up was picking up our mail from the Post Office. I had some papers to print out and sign and get notarized. One was for getting Power of Attorney (POA) over the investments that George had put in his name only. This was early on in his dementia, an early symptom. I had sent all the paperwork in before we left, but they called and said the notary had put his name instead of my name on the "Agent" line. So they needed the whole thing done over again.

I also had an addendum on a real estate offer that I needed to attend to.

At the library, George hovered until I told him to go find the magazine section.

Carbondale has a population of fewer than four thousand. Yet their library is top-notch.

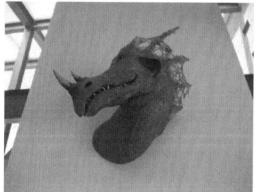

After printing a lot of documents out at the library, we walked over to Wells Fargo. Again they gave us free notary service. THANK YOU WELLS FARGO!

We went exploring by car today. We took Hwy 133 West.

We came to Redstone and I pulled over when I saw these ... things.

It turns out they were ovens for turning the coal mined into the coal that people used to heat their homes and make energy. These "Coke" ovens are being restored.

There was a ranch behind the ovens. I watched a man working his horse. The man said he was "working the spirit out of this horse." He was walking it in circles, then straight, then in circles.

Redstone is now a bedroom community and tourist destination. A big motel used to be housing for the bachelor workers. It is now a high-priced resort and restaurant.

We walked the main street in town which had several art stores and touristy shops.

Ha! The horse trainer was teaching the horse to go down streets with cars and people. The horse's eyes were wide. I tried to keep my distance, but the trainer tried to come close. Then my eyes got wide as I scooted away.

Hwy 133 follows the landscape created by the Crystal River.

317

I saw a sign for Marble a few miles up the road.

Marble was built around the business of mining… you guessed it…Marble! The old factory ruins are now a 25-acre historical park.

Marble slabs for picnic tables.

This marble was used in the Lincoln Memorial in Washington, DC.

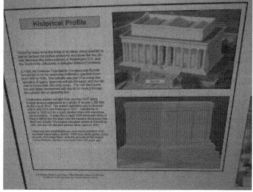

As we were about to get back in our car we saw a yellow-bellied marmot. These are the guys that hibernate seven or eight months a year in the Rocky Mountains.

Later at dinner in Redstone, we watched the humming birds at the feeder and a young couple with a 10-month old baby.

"I am glad I don't have little kids," said George.

"Have I told you how much I love you yet today?" he asked.

Back at our home base, we spent a few minutes out on the back porch, me with my computer, George with a book. Then the darkness and mosquitoes chased us in.

Day 59 was full of awesome engineering. Glenwood Canyon Trail and road make me proud to be an American. What a glorious trail to ride!

A New Financial Perspective

The day starts with a big "Ouch!"
I had to write two big checks.
One to our accountant for preparing last-years taxes. This is another reason to sell the rental properties that aren't making money and make our tax preparation so complicated.
The other check was to a vendor for the business we sold in the fall of 2014. The vendor didn't bill us, or the invoice got lost in the mail or something. But they did the work for our company back at least five months before we sold the business. Now, they noticed they haven't been paid and they want to get paid.
They had contacted me about 14 months after the work was done, and I asked their bookkeeper to find out about giving us a discount because they didn't contact us about this earlier and we had sold the business. Another seven months passes without any contact from her or anyone at their company. Now she contacts me and she asks why I haven't paid yet. I tell her again to find out about the discount. She finally gets back to me this week with a 15% discount.

But, hey, I am looking at the bright side. Both of these bills together aren't as much as it costs to spend a month in the nursing home.

That is my new perspective these days.

The costs of care

With a progressive dementia, if George lives long enough, (which he probably will because he is so physically healthy), there will be a time when one person cannot care for him.

Assisted living and memory care can run from about $2,000 to $4,000 a month. But there is a point when a patient may need more care than provided in assisted living. That is when they need nursing care and that is when the bill bumps up to $8,000 to $13,000 a month... A MONTH!

I have heard of people surviving in nursing care for 10 years or longer with dementia... TEN YEARS!

The fact is those with Alzheimer's most likely will have symptoms such as fear, paranoia, wandering, loss of mobility and insomnia. It requires twenty-four hour care that one person alone cannot provide. Though many try, it is humanly impossible. Most often they end up in a care facility toward the end.

This is always at the back of my mind these days. Budgeting to make our money last used to be a doable project. Now I have no clue how to do this. How do you plan for $8,000 a month when your income is half of that?

I think I have gone off my financial "rocker."

What can I do?

We go on a trip. We go for a bike ride!

Glenwood Canyon Trail

YES we do! On **Day 59** we ride on one of the most fabulous trails in the country, if not the world.

I pack a snack and have George fill our waters, and I drive us about 12 miles to Glenwood Springs, Colorado.

The start of the ride, the trail runs right next to Interstate 70 at the same level. So if you are only going a mile or so, the trail might disappoint you. But go longer, and the delightful engineering begins.

Below is a tunnel for the railway that also makes its way through this canyon.

The interstate goes into tunnels and the bike trail crosses over the highway on a bridge.

Entering the turn to the bridge it is clear that erosion can be a constant maintenance issue on some areas of the trail.

Now we have pulled away from the highway and the noise of the traffic is gone. We are now riding near the Colorado River.

The trail shares several waysides with the interstate. Flush toilets, nice buildings, kiosks and access to the Colorado River.

The interstate took twenty years to design and build. The design process included public input and a strong dedication to maintaining the environmental significance of the gorge and the river that runs through it.

Trees and bushes were planted. Where blasting of the rock occurred, they stained it to match the look of the surrounding rock.

In some areas, to prevent having to blast away walls of rock, they layered the highway's east and westbound lane and the trail. In places the trail runs under the eastbound lane of the interstate.

At one point we stopped to watch rafters go over some whitewater.

You would think, being this close to traffic, the sound would be bothersome. But it wasn't the sound of the highway over our heads that we heard; it was the sound of the river below us.

The trail ends at a parking area with a pit toilet.

I look at my iPad and find another trail further down the road that leads to a town with restaurants. I ask George if we should go.

"Yes." he said.

We ride on the road six more miles to a trail.

The trail takes us to Gypsum where we stop at the first restaurant we come to.

They have the TV on to Fox news and the Republican convention. The waitress rants about the news. I hear the anger in her voice and know it represents the anger in so many. I mention this because it seems to me this election period has some historical significance.

I forgot my purse! Fortunately George had enough cash to cover the meal and a small tip.

We head back toward our car.

I ask George if he has to use the toilet each time we pass one.

"No," he says and shakes his head.

Back in Carbondale we shower and I pack up a backpack. I look all over for the envelopes with the checks that I had written this morning. I had put them in my bike trunk thinking I would mail them somewhere on our bike ride. They must have fallen or blown away.

So I had to re-write the checks. We walked to the Post Office.

Rosie arrived home and said there is free music in Glenwood on Wednesday nights at 7 p.m. Hopefully we will have the energy to go there and do that.

While I was writing this, George came up and scratched my back, "How ya doin'?" he asked. I know this writing is taking time away from him. I take a break and we go through the exercises.

YES! This is our **60th Day** of our 40th Anniversary Celebratory Adventure.

George does yoga with me and afterward agrees with me that it feels good.

We walked to the grocery store and got some food to make salad.

We took a short ride on the trikes.

I said to George, "Well, if we go to Glenwood Springs for the music in the park, we can get ice cream there."

He didn't say anything but looked disappointed.

"You want ice cream now?" I asked.

"Ice cream now, yes," he said.

"OK!" I said. I couldn't find any ice cream shop on my iPad. Locals directed us to Fatbellys.

Oh, what a name! I am feeling guilty and I haven't even taken a lick yet.

"Death by Chocolate."

Later in the day I asked George if he wanted to go to Glenwood Springs for the music or go to the library and watch a movie on his iPad.

"Watch a movie," he said. The library was open until 8:00. We arrived there about 6:45 p.m. He watched a movie, and I went to the Meetup web site and tried to join groups with similar interests to ours and see if there was anything we could attend while we are in Boulder. If we don't get some social life, I will get homesick. I need to find some people to talk to and with whom to do biking and hiking and eating and music listening.

Back at "home" we sat in the spare room, me on the floor and George on the trundle bed.

After a bit, I noticed George wasn't there anymore... but in his place was a wet spot on the bed about seven inches in diameter.

George was in the bedroom laying on the bed reading. His pants weren't wet. "What happened," I asked. "How come the bed in the other room is wet?"

He just looked at me and chuckled.

"Did you have an accident? Did you pee your pants?" I asked.

"Yes," he said.

"How come your pants aren't wet now?" I asked.

He struggled a minute to talk and then was able to tell me, "I changed them."

"Please tell me when this happens," I said. "We can't have this happening on people's furniture. Tomorrow we are getting pads and you are going to wear them."

He nodded.

I took the sheets off the trundle bed and then I went upstairs and told Rosie that he had dementia and a new symptom had shown up... incontinence.

She was in the middle of doing her own laundry, so she said she would take care of it.

When I returned to our bedroom George said, "I'm sorry."

I hugged him, "This is not your fault. That part of your brain has gone missing. You have always been such a clean man. I still love you very much."

"I love you too," he said.

As I lay trying to go to sleep, I wondered, do I cancel the rest of our trip plans? Do we go home now? Confusion... clear... confusion... clear.

Haven't we seen and done enough? Are we still having fun?

Tomorrow we pack up and head to Boulder where we will be in one place for a full ten days. I will see how I feel in a few days.

Day 61 - Pads are on!

July 21, 2016

There was really only one way through the mountains, Interstate 70. This took us back through Glenwood Canyon! Awesome!!!

Neither of us had ever been to Vail, Colorado.

Entering the street from the parking structure I commented it was like Disney for adults. There was a bus stop with tile artwork.

We stopped at the Welcome Center and got directions to coffee and a Gondola ride.

We walked toward the recommended coffee shop.

We watched the crow succeed in getting all the goodies out of the sealed box.

Two twelve ounce cups of coffee and one croissant.... $16!

After enjoying our coffee while watching someone give fly fishing lessons, we headed toward the gondola rides.

There were bike trails all over.

Two tickets for a gondola ride was $58.

While in line we watched the staff load one bike per gondola. People were riding the gondola up to bike around and then down the mountain.

The woman in front of us had a Sanibel Island T-shirt on. I asked if they were from Florida. No, they were from the Chicago area. "We are from Rockford, Illinois originally," I told them.

We ended up in the same car as them.

Another couple joined us in the car. I asked where they were from. "Bloomington, IL," she said.

"WOW," I said, "An Illinois car!"

I mentioned that we had lived in Waukesha, Wisconsin for many years. He said he was friends with Les Paul! (Les Paul the famous electric guitar inventor was from Waukesha, WI.) He said he was working on hearing aids and he would go visit Les Paul once a month for many years.

"The guy was so cheap.... brilliant but cheap." He said they would work late into the night and then at midnight or 2 a.m. Les would heat hotdogs and Velveeta Cheese in the microwave.

George was smiling a lot. When I had first asked about a gondola trip earlier in our travels, he said no. Today, he said yes and he really enjoyed it.

We were so surprised when we got off to find a mini-city at the top. A restaurant, flush toilets, bus tours and more...

We were standing around amazed when my phone rang. It was Jodie, George's daughter!

Here we are on the top of a mountain on a beautiful day and we are chatting with our daughter. So happy.

Ropes and ladders for kids...

And adults...

There was another gondola about one mile away. We walked over to that to go back down the mountain.

Back down in town, we used the restroom.... well I used the restroom. George refused.

We followed signs over to Ford Park.

The nature center was growing gorgeous vegetables.

.Our gondola tickets lasted all day, but we had places to go and a lunch in Vail would be much too expensive.

I pulled off the highway in Frisco.

We found a place to get pizza for $13. We clicked glasses. Happy 61st day of travel.

Leaving Frisco the sky was threatening more rain, but it was only sprinkling. We entered a long tunnel.

When we emerged it was pouring rain.

Down toward Denver ....

Our lodging for the next ten days is in a residential area. Our abode has its own private entrance, bath and kitchenette.

With a "Take your Shoes Off" policy, I had George stay indoors and I took several trips to the car to unload all the things I had brought for a longer stay in one place with a kitchen.

Then I showed him the pads and how to tape them into his underwear.

There are a few stairs between the bedroom and the bathroom. Not a good idea.

I asked George what time it was. 7:00 he told me.

"Wow! Are you hungry again?" I asked.

He nodded enthusiastically.

While I started to make salad, he hovered. I stopped what I was doing and logged him in to the internet on his iPad. That worked to get him out of the kitchen.

While we were eating, George looked a bit sad and ... well mad. I asked him how he was doing.

"Fine," he said. I continued to look at him and then he started looking like he was going to cry.

I tried to get him to talk. He couldn't or wouldn't. So I changed the subject.

I said, "You had a gondola ride today!"

"Twenty years ago you never would you have thought you would stand on top of a mountain and talk on a tiny phone to your daughter," I said.

He smiled and nodded.

I worked on the travel notes and George watched a movie on his iPad.

At bedtime he came to bed with his underwear in his hand. I said, "You are going to wear those tonight, yes?"

"No," he said.

He said that he has not wet the bed yet. I got a glimpse of the strong-headed man he used to be. Have I crushed his spirit?

I explained to him that he leaked while sitting next to the bathroom. We can't take a chance that he will wet someone's bed.

He put them on and climbed into bed.

I tossed and turned, read and played solitaire. I finally got up and worked on this journal. It is now 4:00 a.m.

I guess I should go try and get some sleep.

Day 62 – 63 Introduction to Boulder

After a couple cups of coffee, I study the maps. We will just ride and explore.

Our little apartment does not have air conditioning. It is already getting hot in there by the time we are ready to head out. We close the place up hoping it will conserve what little bit of cool we have.

We are located in a quiet residential area close to bike trails and right on a bike route.

In a few blocks we are on a trail. There are several intersections with other trails and we have to stop often so I can study the map again.

We come upon a traveler. I ride with him a short while. He is from Texas and has been traveling for six years living on his bike. We talked about the joy of the simple life.

347

He had the odor of someone who has lived on his own on a bike in hot weather....

His name was Matt and his little dog is Alfie. I asked if he wrote in order to finance his journey. He said no, but today he was going to go downtown on the mall and play music and put his hat out and see if he could make some money that way. It was his first time trying this.

I wished him luck. Then I had to move over due to bike traffic and our conversation ended.

George and I stopped in the shade so I could study the map. We were right next to a pre-school. The kids came running. So cute!

The kids asked a million questions and then "Why." The boy with the baseball cap said he could run real fast, "Watch," he said.

He took off and the others all said, "I can run fast, watch me!"

Then they came back and showed us how high they can jump.

I stopped at a tourist info place and got maps and the info lady told us where the grocery stores were and things we might do.

We headed toward the Whole Foods market.

348

We took the groceries home and we made ourselves cheese and veggie sandwiches for lunch. Then I chopped up some of the veggies and used some of the stuff I brought from home and have been hauling all this way to make a pot of chili.

George chopped the onion for me. Then he quietly surfed and read.

We have kitchen chairs and a table which is great for eating and working on the computer. We have a comfortable bed. We even have a bench outside in the shade. What we don't have is a comfy place to sit and watch videos or read.

Jodie called. She said she had some bad news. I braced myself. She said she had been investigating and found that George's sister had died in February this year.

We had suspected she was gone. We knew she had dementia and the last we heard she could no longer swallow. After our search for her in Rockford,

349

Jodie had kept searching for her aunt's name and finally it came up with a birth and death date and a funeral home. Jodie asked how George was doing.

Jodie said she was following our journal so she knew some of the dementia symptoms that we were experiencing. George was standing right next to me while I was on the phone, looking at me. I told her he was doing well, but he looked sad and was fighting tears right then.

I said he was sad over the news and sometimes sad over the symptoms of his illness and its progression.

He talked with Jodie for a bit on the phone. Well, he listened and gave short answers.

After he got off the phone, we hugged and he shed a few tears for a little while. Then he blew his nose and was ready for the rest of our day.

I had done a lot of hunting on the internet for social clubs where we could go and meet people. A whole month on our own without people to chat with seems like torture to me.

I found on Meetup a group that was meeting that night in Longmont, Colorado at a downtown free music event. Great! I joined the group and RSVP'd.

The leader said she would be there, up front by the band, with a yellow flag.

I found a great parking spot and we walked to the location of the event.

We got a good spot in view of the band. It would be easy to spot the yellow flag.

We were half an hour early. The event starts at 5:30 and the band starts at 6:00. We watched people and ate our snacks and drank our waters.

5:30 came… no yellow flag...

6:00 came and the lead band played. No yellow flag.

I went around to groups of people who were talking to each other and told them I was looking for the Longmont Social Club. No one knew of the group, but a few said they were social and we were welcome to join them. I should have taken them up on the offer. Instead I kept searching and waiting.

The lead band started.

I told George I missed our friend Frankie. She can really dance to this kind of music. He agreed. He was smiling and tapping his foot.

I kept thinking, if only I had brought my iPad with me. I could have checked the website. Maybe the Meetup leader had forgotten the flag and I could contact the leader and find out where they were sitting. But my iPad was in the car several blocks away.

The sky started to look threatening with lightning. George was ready to leave. At 7:30 we headed back to the car. Before we drove off, I checked my iPad and the Meetup group.

The leader HAD forgotten the flag.

I was REALLY BUMMED.

It rained hard on our drive back to Boulder. We had left our trikes out in the fenced yard. They were wet now. Our apartment was hot. We opened all the windows and set the fans on high.

Tomorrow the weather report says it will be 95 degrees and humid.

Day 63 – I SLEPT!!! WELL!!! I woke up refreshed and happy. I greeted George with a kiss and more.

HE WAS HAPPY!! And he was doing well with his old strong voice.

I dropped my camera last night. I tested it several ways and it just would only take black pictures. I planned our bike ride to a Target store to get a new camera and to a laundromat.

Before we took off, I checked the Meetup groups to see if anything was coming up. The same Meetup group was having a potluck tonight in Longmont. This time I won't have to find them in a crowd, I just have to show up at their house. "YES" to that.

I mentioned to George what we were going to do. He put on his tennis shoes and stood waiting. Oh my, I shouldn't mention what our plans are so early in the process. This is something I have to learn.

I have heard from others, who are further in the journey with their spouse with dementia that they don't mention where they are going until it is time to get in the car. They don't mention someone is coming to visit until they have almost arrived. It is something we have to learn to do to spare ourselves and to keep our loved one calm.

George waited quietly while I took care of packing for our ride and planning our route.

Off we go. The trail along the creek is busy. There are lots of people cooling off with their feet in the water. It is around 10:00 a.m. and already the sunny areas are uncomfortably hot.

At Target I got a camera again!

And a watch... George paid for it out of his wallet. It feels more like a gift that way, even though it all comes from the same pot.

Hey Abby! What do you think of that! The polish is for you, girl! (Abby is my granddaughter. We used to paint our toenails when we played together. When I saw her on this trip she asked me how come I am not painting my toes anymore. So... for her, I now have purple toes.)

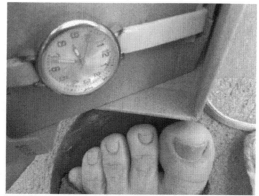

We biked to the end of the Creek Trail before we went to do laundry.
Mr. Potato Head was in the same place he was yesterday -- waving as we passed by.

There were LOTS and LOTS of people using their own tubes to travel down the creek. They used the trail to get back up stream making it hard for us to get going without slowing and stopping for pedestrians. That was okay. Lots of ... interesting ... back-end views.

While in the laundromat, I got into Meetup again and signed us up for two more events - a music one and a hike.

Before we arrived home I stopped at a drug store for toilet paper and next door was a liquor store.

I put two bottles in a laundry bag, and the rest I stuffed in my trunk. I was pleased with myself and smiled big at George.

"You are resource," he said. He had to repeat it several times before I understood his rapid mumble.

"I am resourceful?" I asked.

"Yes," he said.

Just as we pulled in at "home" we heard a thunderclap.

I reheated the chili to take to the potluck tonight.

I was in the kitchen starting to pack up stuff and thinking about when to leave for the potluck. When they say, 6:30 in Boulder, do they mean arrive at 6:30? Eat at 6:30? Arrive at 7:00?

I heard a crash. I rushed to check on George. He was sitting at the bottom of the stairs.

As he was trying to get up, his stocking feet were slipping on the polished wood floor.

I don't know how to fix this. This is not my property, but when I took my first steps down those stairs, I suspected it would be a problem.

ALZHEIMER'S TRIPPIN' with George

1) Slippery

2) You have to remember to hang on to the railing

3) In the middle of the night you have to remember the stairs are there. The stairs are between the bed and the bathroom.

I asked George several times if he was okay. "Did you hurt your butt? Your back? Your ribs?"

"No, no, no," he insisted.

At 6:30 we were on the road in the van heading for Longmont, CO. That is about 15 miles away. After a few minutes of driving George said, "I am fine."

I was kind of wondering how the evening would go. It is different being social at home. People knew George before his dementia. Now they will be meeting him for the first time, and he won't be saying much.

Before we even got into the house, I introduced us to a guy who was going in at the same time, Scott. Later he would come by and chat with us at length.

We walked through the house; the party was in the backyard. The brick area is the grill where two guys were cooking burgers and brats.

We arrived at around 6:50 and people were eating. So we didn't arrive too early. George was hungry. I asked him if he wanted to make up a cheese sandwich with the bun and cheese.

Yes. So I got him a plate and showed him were the cheese was. There were all these things right in front of him, but he didn't notice them. The mustard, the lettuce and slices of red vine-ripened tomatoes were all there.

When he turned around he had a bun with cheese and a sliver of onion. I took him back and helped him dress his sandwich. I showed him the other dishes available. There was Jello salad, broccoli salad, cucumber salad, my chili and chips.

Then I needed a place to sit him. There were no more chairs available at the tables. He would not succeed at balancing a plate on his knee. We walked around a bit until a seat opened up and I had him sit there.

Then I went to fill my plate and chat with folks.

The first person I sat and chatted with I told about our journey through the USA and through dementia symptoms. She was very supportive.

I didn't tell anyone else about the dementia. It may have been obvious... I don't know.

Later I got a chair next to George at the table. The guy across from us (Gerry) was drinking a beer with an interesting label. He said it is made in Loveland, CO (nearby).

Gerry has a stone shop near Loveland. I got his card and we will stop in there on one of our drive days.

This event was a potluck and movie. Steve had a blowup movie screen.

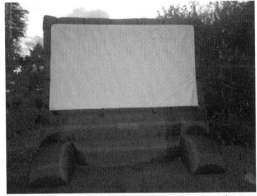

The mosquitoes began to bite just before the movie started. I asked George if he wanted to go. He nodded and started to walk toward the door.

"Wait, we have stuff to pack up," I said.

When we were packed up, we went to introduce ourselves to the host of the event. We were stopped briefly a couple of times by people who had not met us yet, but had heard from others that we were traveling and had joined the Meetup for the month we would be here.

"I wanted to let you know that I think what you are doing is awesome," one woman said.

When we got home, George was getting ready for bed. I checked to see if he had changed his underwear since he started wearing pads. He had not. So I got out a clean pair and put a pad in it and told him to take the old ones off.

Later I checked and he had the new ones on and he had put the old pad in the waste basket. Good.

Day 64 - Living without a Plan

In the morning I worked on checking our accounts, responded to email, drafted a newsletter for the bike group back home.

I got lovely emails from friends supporting us on our journey. One friend wrote she was looking forward to our return, so we could ride and eat together. She sent hugs.

Another friend who is becoming a caretaker for her husband with Alzheimer's wrote (I have changed the names to protect their identity),

"You are my hero!

Am following your travels and look forward to it each day. You give me hope for the "right now" and an insight into what's next. Bob hasn't had any serious issues with incontinence except when he had the UTI. For that I am grateful.

I have a hard time dealing with the lack of communication as he doesn't remember from morning to afternoon what took place. Being together more causes me to think up activities that we can do together. Our daytime dates consist of grocery shopping, Wal-Mart, and Culvers. Sometimes we drive to the dump with yard waste. It is a different life.

I still go to exercise and line dancing during the week. I need the social aspects of this too. I miss having someone to walk with.

You and George are fortunate in that you enjoy the same things. I am thankful that at this stage Bob is agreeable to do most anything I come up with, but I do have to watch out for things that would tire him as then he doesn't do well. He turned 80 on July 7th....

I see, as you do, that some days are better than others.

Just wanted you to know that my thoughts are with you both and I admire what you are doing. ...

Take care and be safe. Thanks for sharing this journey."

George surfed Facebook and news on his iPad, and then he came and just sat watching me work.

ARG! I feel rushed. I feel like I should be doing something with him. I feel I have to plan an activity. I can't just have a day to get stuff done!

I keep working. Later, George is looking sad.

I decide I will work on planning our week later. We needed to get out and enjoy today.

First we had to eat because it was already almost noon.

I made taco salads with the leftover chili and veggies.

Then we slathered on the sun screen and pulled our bikes out for a ride.

361

I didn't know where we were going. I figured we would just follow the bike routes and bike lanes and bike paths. And when we had about 20 miles in I would pull out my iPad and map our way back home.

Easy-peasy! No plan, just go.

I stopped at a playground and did bench dips and pushups. George and I climbed up this rope ladder and tried to do some modified pull-ups. Then the kids showed up, so we got down and let them have it.

I told George, "We need to have an adult play ground in our neighborhood."

When I saw a little figure on a trail information kiosk, I had to turn around and take a picture. As I was taking this picture a glider went right above the treetops over our heads.

"Did you see that?" I asked George. He smiled big and nodded.

Sometimes when you travel without knowing the area and without a plan... you come to dead ends...

After lunch George rinsed his spoon and asked where to put it. I said, "Let's have you do all the dishes, not just your spoon." I filled the serving bowl with soapy water, and I stacked all the dirty dishes on the tiny counter space next to the sink.

He washed and rinsed and placed in a drying rack. I dried. It worked! I just needed to re-train him on how to do the dishes.

This happened at home too. He would just walk up to the sink and rinse a dish, instead of preparing the area by stacking the dirty dishes in one area and then filling a container with soapy water. Sometimes I show him how, and it sticks for a long time before he forgets the process again.

After dinner we went for a walk.

I wanted to get postcards. I remembered that George used to draw a character when he was in the Navy. I asked George if he remembered how to draw it, and he said he did.

I said he could color the post cards himself instead of us sending a picture.

I found some note-cards that will work.

Back at our "home" I pulled out the colored pencils we had packed on the trip. George colored four cards before he got tired of it and went to watch a movie on his iPad.

Tomorrow, we will drive up to Estes Park. We will probably stop in Loveland at the stone shop we learned about last night. We have to get it all done before 6:00 because there is a meetup in Longmont again... music!

Too much for one day? We will go with the flow.

365

Day 65 - Estes Park and Dancing

What a day full of awe and beauty! Today we went to Estes Park.

First I sent an email to Arlene in Broomfield confirming that we had arrived in the area and still planned on cat and house-sitting for her starting this coming weekend. I asked when we could come by to get instructions and meet Gus the cat.

I made our picnic lunch. It was after nine by the time we loaded up the car and left for the day.

As we were entering Estes Park the town, I got a call and I pulled into a city park. It was Arlene who arranged for us to come by and meet Gus, the cat, on Thursday night at 7:00.

The lake at the park was crystal clear. George and I used this beautiful spot to go through some of his exercises. I have been neglecting this daily routine.

We stopped in the visitors' center and the clerk was hospitable but it was clear she was burned out. She pointed out that the Bear Lake parking lots were already full, so we won't be able to get in there.

She said we would probably enjoy the Alluvial Flow. Alluvial... ?? What's that?

The information center had free shuttle buses. The next one was leaving at 10:30. It was 10:00.

So here is my dilemma. I SAY I am environmentally conscious. I THINK of myself as an environmental advocate. No herbicides, natural landscaping, ride your bike and walk, energy efficiency and all that.

But I didn't want to wait a half hour.

It was clear that someday soon they would have to make bus travel the mandatory way to travel within Estes National Park. There were a LOT of people at the info center and a LOT of cars in the parking lot.

I drove. There were three lanes of traffic going into Estes National Park.

We stopped at the Alluvial Flow. We approached without knowing what it was. It appears there was a flash flood and it pushed a bunch of huge rocks and sand down the mountain.

We parked and hiked in, picking our way over the rocky path.

Not far in we found a beautiful waterfall and a huge area of rock.

See the tiny people in the picture above?

Later a kiosk explained that an old dam up on the mountain had some old caulking fail. And the water came rushing down bringing with it rock that loosened up more rock and trees.

It then overwhelmed the dam in a lake at a lower elevation and that broke. Finally a third dam held. That saved the city and residents of Estes Park.

This occurred in 1982, over thirty years ago.

We are learning and experiencing and smiling a lot.

I had thought that if we take the narrow, gravel road to the top, we would be among just a few other adventurous travelers.

But there was a steady stream of cars. I would pull over and let some pass because I wanted to go slow and enjoy the ride..

And sometimes, with steep drop-offs I was making moaning, whining sounds that made George laugh.

Each switchback, each time we came around a curve a new and awesome sight had me saying over and over, "Oh my!" and "Wow!" and "Isn't that beautiful?" and "I got to stop and take a picture."

But the pictures came out bleached out and flat. Like this picture of a falls across the valley...

I was getting hungry. At one switchback I saw a large trail. I parked and we grabbed our lunch and my camera and headed for the trail.

Looking back at our car parked at the switchback.

We soon came upon a lodge. The sign posted said it was a federal building and doing damage to it was a federal offense.

371

And in front of the building was a picnic table with a beautiful vista over a flower covered meadow!

After lunch we walked down to the creek. I started moving rocks around to adjust the flow of the creek. I could have played like that for hours. George tossed a couple rocks, and then just stood and watched.

OK, time to keep moving...

As we traveled further up the road in the car we saw a yellow bellied marmot.

I stopped the car and wondered. You are not supposed to bother the wildlife. Then the little guy ran TOWARD our car. Now, I couldn't see it. Was it under the car? Was it in front of the wheel? Did it already pass to the other side of the road?

I started creeping forward real slow and the marmot ran out to just two feet to the side of the driver's door. Naughty tourists must be feeding it.

At the top, we would come into the Visitor Center. This is the same visitors' center we had been to with my brother, Larry. We had approached from the other side of the mountains last time.

The parking lot was FULL. People were parked along the road. Rangers or volunteers were out helping direct traffic. I found a spot. I just wanted to re-fill our waters. I used the restroom. I asked George.

"No," he said and shook his head.

There was a steady stream of tourists climbing to the top of the hill and taking selfies like George and I had done a week before.

There are a few bikers now on the road. Many of them we see resting at pull-out areas and scenic overlooks. They look spent.

We saw elk and stopped to take pictures. George pulled out his camera and I helped him find the right lens.

George's camera zoomed in on the Alluvial Flow we had stopped at earlier in the day.

I had thought that we had seen all the beauty there was to see. We were on our way down and out of the park...

But the scenery was always changing and each scene was unique and.... well, just one more picture...

After leaving the park we went through a beautiful gorge. I took pictures while driving. "WOW!" "Awesome!"... "Cool!"

MILES OF SMILES!!!

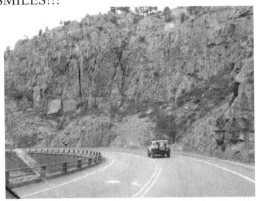

We entered Loveland and right away found the Blue Stone store.

I studied the earrings a while and then walked around the shop. A window looks out on a deck ... with a peacock.

Gerry, the owner we met at the Meetup group was there. He explained that the peacock arrived with two hens two years ago.

Then I saw some feather shaped items with a wire wrap. They are made of bone by a local Native American woman.

I got a necklace and earrings. I put them on right away. $101.

George said, "Happy Anniversary!"

Thank you, George! I love them.

The Longmont Social Club was meeting at a park for another free music concert. We went right there... the park is at 2011 100-Year-Party Court. I am not kidding you. I put the address in my navigator and it found it right away!

Steve who had hosted the potluck had told me he would display the US flag so we could find them. Yeah! We found it.

People from our group were dancing. I got up and danced too. We waved goodbye to the group at the last song.

Day 66 – 67 The Joys of Daily Living

Day 66 we didn't do anything special. No tourist activities or sight-seeing. I just took care of business. Yay!!

George... George, I think, just surfed the net. One day I sat next to him as he was going through Facebook. I thought he would click on my blog and look at the pictures. He just paused and then continued to scroll.

I called and left a message for the Realtor in Alabama. If we were closing tomorrow, how come I hadn't any paperwork yet to sign and return?

LaterI heard back from the title company. The gal at the title company had dropped the ball. She sent me the paperwork via email right then.

I mentioned to George that after I was done taking clothes out of the dryer we would have to go to the library and print things out.

With the anticipation that we were going to go do something, George pulled the trikes out and sat in the driveway on his trike for quite a while.

We rode over to the library which was only three blocks away.

I had questions about the documents, and I had not brought the title company contact info with me. We went back to our "home" so I could read the documents over and call her with questions.

By this time it was noon and George was hungry. We were out of bread. I put peanut butter on a plate and pulled out the carrots and fruit. We snacked on that while I reviewed the documents.

George waited in the driveway again while I cleaned up and got ready to go.

First the bank for a notary and then UPS to send it back to the title company. Then we rode to the Post Office to pick up our mail.

I told George that we would drive to Fort Collins, CO tomorrow and visit the bike shop and ride the trails there. When we arrived back home we put the trikes in the van, ready to go.

On **Day 67** we went to Fort Collins to ride the Poudre Trail.

At one point we turned off the trail and rode toward the historic downtown "square."

We stopped in the info shop and got a map of the bike trails in Fort Collins. We also got directions to the Post Office.

At the Post Office there was a long line. I used a machine to buy postage... only instead of getting little stamps it printed out big labels! They didn't fit in the space I had available on the postcards. Now that is DUMB!

I would wait to find a small-town Post Office and get little stamps for the post cards.

We got back on the trail.

At the end of the trail was another trail.

The little trail ended in a small town...
...with a small Post Office....
... with small post card stamps.

Back on the Poudre trail we crossed a strange bridge. It turned the corner in the river and took us down the river a bit before taking us back on land.

At each end of the bridge was a warning to stay on the trail and respect private property with fines and statute sited. There must be an UN-cooperative land-owner who didn't want to allow trail easement.

We were both happy to get home.

Day 68 – 69 Hike, Ride, I lost my keys!

I had signed us up for a three-mile Newcomers hike through Meetup.com. It started at 7:30 a.m. at Chautauqua. .

We were to meet at the Ranger Station. I was a bit apprehensive that:

I wouldn't be able to find the Ranger Station, and George would not be able to keep up with the group.

We drove in and the first parking lot was by the Ranger Station! I am relieved, and then right away we met a couple of people who were also going on the hike. Great!

The ranger came out and distributed trail maps. Seeing the many trails through the area, I was glad we were going with a guide.

She explained that way back in the late 1800's Boulder decided to set aside open space around the town and began buying up land for open spaces. The city has a sales tax to fund this. It is now about 8.8 cents on a $10 purchase.

We started the hike uphill.

The "Flatirons" behind her came off the Rocky Mountains and over time were moved here... A LOT of time...

She stopped often and talked. At one point as she was talking I saw a cloud swirling and descending over one of the Flatirons.

Then the next time I looked it was clear blue sky.
And then it did it again. All in a matter of three to five minutes or so.

George was keeping up very well. He was ahead of me!

Back at our home base after the hike, we walked over to the shopping center and library just a few blocks from "home."

I found the "books for sale" section and picked out two books. When we got back "home," George started reading the fun one...

At about 3:00 p.m. we went to the Leanin' Tree Museum.

Leanin' Tree is a company that makes greeting cards. This is their private collection.

Then we drove over to where we will start our house-sit on Sunday.

We met Arlene and Dick and Gus. Gus the cat took right away to George, and Arlene was surprised and pleased.

Dick showed me all his flowers and indoor plants and told me about the watering schedule. I took notes. I would hate to kill a plant while they are gone.

They have a security system, and I know that will be interesting getting used to it.

In the morning of **Day 69** I pulled out my computer to journal our trip.

While I was writing, George came out several times and asked how I was doing. He was anxious to get going.

It was 9:00 a.m. when I had George fill our water thermoses and take the trikes out of the van.

The shoulder goes away and the climb gets steeper. I am in my lowest gear and still sometimes I stop to rest.

Boulder's open spaces reach beyond the city and they also have open spaces in the mountains.

We found that NO cars obeyed this sign.

We pulled over in the shade and took a good look at the scenery.

We came to a scenic overlook, and I was excited because I drank a lot of water and coffee and I needed the facilities.

There were no facilities.

We got back on our trikes and continued to climb. I saw a building up around the next switchback.

There was one truck in the lot.

I walked to the building and discovered it wasn't a toilet but a picnic area shelter. I went behind it and tried to assess if I could squat in privacy. But I decided against using a picnic area. When I walked out from behind the shelter there was a man unlocking the shelter... right there, around the corner.

"Good thing I waited!" I said to George who was following me.

We made it to the next rest stop, Crown Rock. And GLORY BE! A toilet!

I always ask if George needs to go first.

Usually he says no, this time he said "YES!"

So I danced until it was my turn. When I was done I emerged with my arms raised, triumphant.

I had planned on riding now to NCAR ... National Climate and Atmospheric Research Center. I figured it would not take long because it was all downhill.

We started our descent. At one point I could hear a car screech around a curve behind me. I put out my hand to signal him to slow and wait for the next curve and the ascending cars. Then I put my arm down when the coast was clear and he stepped on the gas.

I didn't have a signal for Verizon so I couldn't map our route to NCAR until we got down into the city again. As I looked at the route I realized that NCAR was up in the foothills. Uphill on a different route!

We started climbing again. I was going just under 3 mph. Diamond frame bicycles would pass us and then a long time later I would see them still pushing it around a curve...

It didn't look steep, but we were in low gear and not moving very fast. It takes a long time to go two miles when you are only going 2 mph... Duhhh. It takes one hour!

I stopped to rest and I asked George how he was doing.

"Fine," he said... "It's a struggle, but I am fine."

It was another half mile of climb around a large curve before we arrived.

We were ten minutes late for the tour. At this point, I didn't care about that. The priority for us was to refill our waters, rest, and refuel.

We had a beautiful view from our picnic spot.

NCAR has major computers that process trillions of bits. They use the computer for modeling weather patterns in all the different levels of our atmosphere but mostly the bottom layer where we live.

I read this panel that explains how they know the atmospheric changes are man-made and not just another normal cycle. Fossil fuel carbon atoms look different and therefore they can track how much of the carbon in the atmosphere is from our fossil fuel use.

I said to George, "And what are we doing? We are driving around the country! Why are we doing this when we know it is bad for the environment?"

We coasted down... down... down... and more down.

I found that we could catch the Banjo Billy's Bus Tour downtown near Pearl Street. Pearl Street is three blocks of pedestrian mall with performers, and kiosks, and fountains.

We had an hour before the bus tour. We walked until we found a coffee shop. I got a tea and George got coffee and we shared a caramel brownie thing...

I have to admit this... in public. The clerk didn't smile. And when he said the price was $4.77, I knew it wasn't right. George's coffee alone was almost $3. But I was tired of paying $9 and $20 for two coffees and a shared pastry. I was tired of high prices. Tired! And that is my excuse for not saying anything.

While we were sitting there I remember taking my keys and tucking them into my waistband on my bike pants. I have no pockets; I do this often. I remember thinking I had them tucked OK, in an area where the bulge wouldn't show through my t-shirt.

Later we sat in front of the Hotel Boulderado where we were supposed to catch the tour bus. It was five minutes before the bus left, and we didn't see any other patrons or the bus. I got up to ask one of the hotel bell-boys when I saw the bus parked around the corner.

I guess "front of the motel" had meaning for those who knew which side was the front.

Anyway, we made it; we were on the bus and glad to be sitting.

After our bus trip we went to the Rio Grande Mexican Restaurant.

When we arrived home, I discovered my keys were not in my trunk or in my bike pant waistband.

I worked on keeping myself calm, so I wouldn't get George excited. I called Banjo Billie's and left a message. I called the Mexican Restaurant, and no one had turned them in.

When George is in the shower I always bring out a new pair of underwear and put a new incontinence pad in them. Today was the first time his pads were full of urine. There must be something in them to keep odors down because I never smelled it. I roll his used pad up and put it in the waste basket and make a mental note to take the trash out tomorrow.

Sometimes I step into his underwear to stretch out the pants as I put the pad in. George stepped out of the shower as I was doing this... "Really, I am not into men's underwear," I say. "This is just easier to do it this way."

He smiles.

Tomorrow my priority will be finding my keys or getting a replacement fob. George had a set of keys, but his fob doesn't work anymore. Maybe a dealer can put a new battery in it...??

I am trying to remain calm. I don't want to lose sleep over it. It will all turn out well in the end.

As I climb into bed, George says, "I still love you anyway."

I say, "In spite of???"

He says, "You losing your keys."

I saw in trusted house-sitters that someone in the UK was looking for someone to watch their Siamese cats for a week in late August. I responded on a whim. What am I thinking!????

I'd like to have our trikes with us if we go. Use them as transportation... What am I thinking!???

Day 70 - Are the keys on the bus????

It is Saturday, July 30, 2016; we have been on the road for 70 days.

In the morning George asked if I had found my keys yet.

"No," I said.

I started gathering stuff up camera, purse, books to give away, letters to mail, laundry to wash. While I was doing that, George went out and moved the trikes from the back yard to the driveway.

Fortunately I had a tube of sun guard on the bikes. The other tube was in the car. We couldn't get in the car...

Then my phone rang. It was a gal from Banjo Billy's Bus Tours. I had called them last night and left a message. Good news, they have my keys!

She said I can meet the bus at the same stop by the Boulderado Hotel at 11:00 a.m. After I hung up, I jumped up and down and cheered.

We arrived way before the bus was scheduled to arrive.

The bus was there already.

I introduced myself to the driver and explained that I had left my keys on the bus and that the office had called me to tell me they were found and in the box on the bus.

I was expecting him to grab them right away and hand them over to me. But he began to look a bit panic-stricken.

"I just got back from vacation last night, I don't know anything about any keys," he said.

I said the gal at the office said...

"Who did you speak with," he interrupted.

Dang, I didn't get a name. I told him it was a young bubbly woman.

He tried to help me out. He looked around. He called the office and texted the guide we had on the bus last night.

But it was soon time for him and his guide to start their show. The bus was filling up with tourists.

He said, "Come back in one and a half hours and we will search more."

Oh man! I was so hoping to be celebrating right now.

George and I walked back down to Pearl Street. I took his hand and told him this was a good excuse to go out to eat for lunch. We went in search of lunch.

Lunch was good. I was pleased. While we sat, I opened my iPad and researched how to change the battery in a Chrysler 2011 mini-van key fob. It seemed simple. I wrote down the kind of battery I needed and researched where there was a Batteries Plus in town. I found one on the google map and I felt relieved that if they didn't find my keys at least I could go there and repair the fob I had given George that was out of power.

After lunch we watched performers on Pearl Street.

I found us a bench in the shade across the street from where the bus stops and kitty-corner from where our trikes were parked. From here I could keep an eye on both corners and be comfortable.

As we sat, I thought it would be good to have my phone in case Banjo Billy's office calls and also, I could call Chrysler and find out about what to do if my key fob really is lost. I had left my phone on my trike.

I told George to stay and I ran across two streets to our trikes and got the phone. As I was walking back across the street toward the bus stop, the bus pulled in. At the same time my phone rang. I answered the phone, and while I talked I was aware that George was up off the bench and watching me.

It was the woman from the bus station calling me again saying that the keys were definitely on the bus and they were put in "the box."

I heard a car horn and saw George crossing the street in his zombie-like gait with his eyes fixed on me. He was walking against the traffic light!

I said, "George!" into the phone and hung up to get him off the street. George smiled.

I said, "George, I am right here. You could see me!"

He just smiled.

I talked to the bus driver again. We looked in "the box" together. Then he asked "Which box did she put it in?"

"I don't know," I said. They could not get a reply back from the woman who guided us last night because she was at a different job.

We didn't find the keys. I was bummed.

He said they might be in a lock box back at the parking lot. I said I could meet them there on my bike and gave him my phone number. He had another tour right away and then a tour at 4:00. He was frustrated too. He finally said, "Ultimately it is not our responsibility."

George and I got on our trikes and headed toward the Batteries Plus Store.

We were almost there when my phone rang. It was the bus driver.

"I got your keys, come back," he said.

"OH WONDERFUL!!!" I hung up and turned around and George followed. I don't even know if George knew I got a call or why I turned around.

I was pushing it to get back. George kept up.

I arrived at the bus; I pulled a twenty out of my purse and plopped it in his hand when he gave me the keys.

"YES! THANK YOU THANK YOU! I am SOOOOO relieved!" I said

I was so excited and relieved, I forgot to ask where and how he found them.

We took off for the laundromat

When we got done we loaded up the laundry on the trikes and I saw a bee on my reflective triangle...

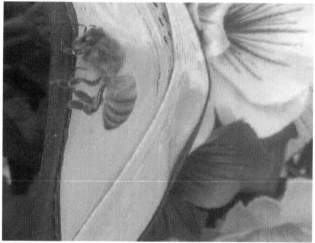

On our way to get ice cream afterward, we passed a neighborhood that looked a LOT like co-housing! I know there is co-housing in Boulder. I remember hearing about it when we were trying to organize co-housing in Wisconsin, years ago.

I made a U-turn to get a closer look.   We rode through the community.

It has a community building. This is used for recreation, meetings and occasional shared meals.

All the homes had solar panels.

This U-shaped neighborhood with the community center in the middle had a playground for the kids.

We finished our neighborhood tour. Then we got ICE CREAM!!!!

We continued to bike for a while exploring.

I deposited books in a free library.

Tomorrow we pack up, clean up, and in the afternoon we will officially have our first house-sitting and cat-sitting gig. I hope we do well.

Last night while looking at the house-sitting gigs, I saw a lovely Siamese that needed sitting and on a whim I responded. I told her we would be finishing our cat sit in Colorado on the 23rd and then could fly to her. She is leaving on the 25th! I even told her that George has beginning Alzheimer's disease and we are traveling.

This morning I got an email back. She is holding the position for me while I figure out flights and decide do we really want to do it.

"Where is it?" you ask.

It is in some small village about 15 miles from Liverpool, England. We have never traveled overseas together.

I will have to check if we have our passports with us... Anyone out there know a cheap tour director that could book us cheap flights????

ALZHEIMER'S TRIPPIN' with George

Day 71 - Adjusting to Changes

We had breakfast in our little Airbnb Boulder "home" for the last time. I laid out the plan to George.

We have to take our shoes off when we enter the apartment. So here is the plan:

We pack up and set everything outside the door.

Then we put our shoes on and put everything in the car.

Then we come back and take our shoes off and clean.

"Sounds like a good plan," he said.

Packing and piling and stuffing the car went well.

We cleaned the kitchen, bathroom, and together we made the bed. George was always a great kitchen cleaner, so he volunteered to do that. He forgot to wipe off the table and the shelf, forgot to clean the fridge. I did it, no problem.

George started to vacuum. We only had one room to vacuum. He vacuumed half of it and thought he was done. I reminded him and he finished the job.

We were in our car and ready to leave and it wasn't even 9:30 a.m.!

We aren't supposed to arrive at our next place until 1:00 p.m.

That is when we will unload our stuff in their garage and put some seats up in our van. We are going to drive Arlene and Dick to the airport.

"We haven't been to Celestial Seasonings yet, let's go there," I suggest.

"Good idea!" says George.

But it wasn't such a good idea. I forgot it was Sunday. It is closed on Sunday.

"How about we go get some coffee and figure out what to do."

We went to Burger King. They had some comfy chairs at Burger King! I was sitting in the tan chair, facing George.

George said, "I am not doing too hot am I?"

I hesitated... "Why do you say that?"

His eyes welled with tears. "I keep forgetting things."

I didn't know what to say. He had noticed how he had forgotten to finish the kitchen cleaning and forgot to vacuum half the room.

He was looking at me so sad. I kept looking away. I didn't know what to say. So much emotion, too much emotion, I didn't know how to react.

"Yes, I can tell it is progressing," I said. "We are powerless to do anything to stop it."

Emotions are getting too intense here. It is okay to look at sad things and feel sad things, but.... I have always tried to swerve away, not dwell there too long.

"All we can do is enjoy the life we have," I say to him. "We have seen some wonderful things on this trip."

"And you are still nice to me," I said.

George smiles through his tears. I get up and sit next to him and hold his hand. We just sit sipping our coffee and holding hands.

George says, "I am glad I am still nice to you."

"Me too," I say and lay my head on his shoulder. "I don't know how I would handle it if you were mean to me."

After a bit we decide to drive up into a canyon. We have time.

We stopped the car at Boulder Falls and watched some people climbing the rock wall...

Can you see them??? Look in the lower right corner of the picture above.

A path was closed. Two people had died climbing. You know how tourists can be...

A new kind of "NO" sign. No drones...

411

After Nederland we headed back down the mountain. Did I neglect to tell you that I figured out how to get into low gear for going down long hills? I am pretty proud of myself.

The mountain had recently had a fire. We saw handmade signs thanking the firefighters. In Nederland the fire house was the biggest and best in the whole town.

We arrived at 12:55 at Arlene and Dicks. Arlene answered the door looking damp from running around trying to get everything done before their flight today.

George and I unloaded our van. There was not enough room in their garage for our trikes. We locked them up in the back yard.

They have a sprinkler system so as we locked them I thought we would have to come up with something better later.

Dick is the gardener. I am going to be taking care of his flowers and plants. I hope the flowers all survive!

At 1:30 we had their stuff loaded and were ready to go.

Arlene told me not to use the GPS because it will take me the wrong way. She would give me directions, she said. Dick said he could give us directions, and she said he can't give directions; he doesn't know which way to go.

413

I pulled forward in the driveway and asked, "OK, so which way do I turn."

And Arlene had to think it through a moment and then told me to turn right. Then they both started talking about things.

Right away I came to a T.

"Which way now?" I asked. They debated, then "Go left."

She then got on her phone and started making calls. In the meantime, Dick is telling us of places to visit during our stay. Stereo voices, such fun!

I am interrupting and saying, "Which way do I turn next."

Such energy in that van! But, you know what? I didn't have to turn around once. Smooth sailing into the airport. They unloaded at exactly 2:10 p.m. which is two hours before their flight exactly.

Bada bing, bada boom!

I use the GPS to get home. It takes us much longer... and it is a lot quieter.

As soon as we got home we moved the trikes up onto the deck so they would be somewhat protected from rain and the sprinklers.

I say.... this is our new "home" now. We will be house and cat sitting for several weeks.

I went through the fridge to find out what items would spoil if we didn't eat them before Arlene and Dick returned.

After making the salad, I went to the computer room to log in to the Wi-Fi and work on the blog.

Which one do I unplug so I can plug in my computer?

Dick collects things... half the garage and two rooms are full of things he collects.

In the computer room, George is sitting on the bed to be next to me. I find a chair and make some space for him.

I send out the newsletter to our bike group back in Florida. I check my email, and I have a contact from Sylvia Halpern of a couple that flies overseas with their trikes. I have "friended" him on Facebook and hope to get some answers.

I talked to George about this opportunity to go to England. He just smiles. I know it isn't something on his bucket list, but I think if we go and trike around he will have a good time. I wonder if I am just doing it now because it is my chance to do it with George.

At this point, I think George just likes being with me and doing and seeing different things. I want to go for it. I email the woman and tell her I am excited.

After supper we take a walk to a grocery store and buy some chocolate and veggies. It was a four-mile walk round trip. While we were there I checked on the price of a bullet blender. I looked for a blender at Arlene's and didn't find one. The cheap bullets are $20.

George did well on the walk. He walked a good clip with no dragging feet or tilted torso.

When we got home, he seemed kind of unsure what to do and stood in the hallway a while.

I was glad to see Gus the cat come out of hiding when we got home and let us pet him. He is still skittish, but he will get used to us in a day or two.

George spent some years in Westminster, which is close to here during his early teen years. Tomorrow I am going to map us a ride to the old part of Westminster. He was there over 55 years ago. We will see if anything looks familiar to him.

Day 72 - Getting Around

Last evening I talked to George about going to England. After thinking about it I realized I would be spending my time in Colorado trying to get everything set up for our trip to England.

I contacted the lady who wanted us to house sit in Kingsley, UK and said to go ahead and hire someone else for the gig. She already had someone picked out in case we didn't come. She understood; her father had Alzheimer's disease.

This morning I felt so tired... so frustrated. I had no plan for our first full day in Broomfield and George was waiting.

I do not have a paper map of the area trails yet. I decided to go check out the community center and see if they had weights and if we could pay per visit. I also decided that we would bike to Westminster. I was frustrated to learn Westminster is 34 miles across and I could not find a "historic downtown."

George went out and filled up the tires on the trikes and then was ready to go.

I had to:

- water the plants outside with fertilized water and I had to clean up the kitchen;
- feed the cat and clean his kitty litter;
- get George to fill the water bottles with ice and water;
- pack an emergency snack; and
- make sure we both got lathered up with sun guard.

A single person does it all themselves without any help. It shouldn't be a problem to do it all. Every time, though, it is a reminder that we used to be a team in such things and now so much of it is up to me.

I also think the stress for me is that George is waiting... watching and waiting... sometimes following me around closely with five inches between us... watching and waiting...

The community center is only about a mile away, easy to get to on a bike.

Wow! It has weights and equipment and classes! They charge $6 per visit per person. When we go I will have to remember to pack George a book and stuff to do because I will want to work out two hours, and he will be done in 45 minutes.

Our next destination was the visitors' center in Westminster. Maybe they could tell us where the old Westminster is located. I also wanted bike maps.

The thing with using the iPad to map our route is I have to hold it in the crook of one arm all the time. It is hazardous going downhill, and occasionally I hit the screen with my breast or my finger and I lose the map I was following.

The area is growing. There is a lot of construction and new houses in Westminster area. Arlene and Dick had told us that modest houses are going for one million dollars. It isn't just the Denver area, but as far away as Longmont I had heard someone getting $65,000 over asking price for their house.

One person said the explosion happened right after the marijuana law passed. I don't know if that is a catalyst. There must be jobs in the area. A person can't buy a home without having a job and money.

The Googlemaps.com routing took us to a dead end! What's with that???

I studied the map a while and then gave up.

It is getting SOOOO HOT! There is hardly any shade at all, anywhere. I am almost out of water.

We started heading back toward businesses and "home."
We went to Zoes for lunch. We got lots of ice water.

After lunch I went looking for:
1) a small blender like a bullet; and
2) a sewing kit so I can put a button back on one of George's pants.

Back home I was investigating where we will go tomorrow... what will we do? "We really can't bike around here when it is so hot and there is no shade," I told George.

We had a smoothie right away and then a few hours later we had another smoothie.

In the evening I thought I should spend some time sitting with George instead of on the computer blogging. I offered to watch a movie with him.

Tomorrow is still up in the air....

Day 73 - Red Rock Amphitheater... SHAZAM!

I woke up feeling rested, but when I got out of bed I was tired. I didn't want to do anything today. George was ready for the day and waiting.

After breakfast and house duties, I tried to find a tourist office that might have bike maps of Denver area. I knew from my earlier research that there are several trails and some interconnect making for a good ride.

But it was going to be 97 today. We will go sightseeing and stop at some tourist centers by car. After yesterday's crazy ride in search of the Chamber of Commerce in Westminster, I lost some trust in my iPad as a bike navigator.

As much as I prepare, as I am pulling out of the drive I realize I forgot the sun screen and I forgot to bring a change of pants for George in case we hike and he has an accident.

I do not pull back in to get those things. The alarm on the house is turned on; it is too complicated and scary to go back in and out.

I take us to the Info Center in Arvada, Colorado.

The info center didn't have any bike trail maps. She gave us a map of downtown Arvada. The Info Center sits next to the two or three blocks that are the historic downtown area.

Now the GPS is set to direct us to the Red Rock Amphitheater and to avoid the freeways please...

We took the stairs up out of a parking area. I stopped every once in a while to catch my breath.

"The air is sure thin up here," George said.

We entered another parking lot and learned that the trail we were on would take us to the Amphitheater.

There it is! Wow!

We learned it holds 10,000 people. Its size was impressive. We stood for a while taking it in. We saw that there were people running up the stairs and down the stairs, running back and forth in the seating section, and up and down the seating section. Some would stop and do push-ups, planks, dips... They weren't part of a class. It was just individuals or a few friends, getting some great exercise.

As we started walking up the stairs, we saw they were preparing for the show tonight and using a skid pulled by a cord to get equipment up to the projection room.

I took a picture of this guy in tights because of his cool tights and his long lean legs.

Later we saw him run up the bleachers, then going back down he would jump sideways into a deep squat each step down.

As we climbed the stairs we paused to catch our breath, watching all the athletes running up and down and feeling a bit old and out of shape. Then a little woman going down with her family started singing...."When I get old and losing my hair..." Exactly! We laughed.

Red Rocks is, directly west of Denver.

Even before they built the amphitheater there were performers that would come and use this spot because of the great acoustics.

The number of performers each year has increased. In 1969 I noticed Dionne Warwick, Joan Baez, and Peter, Paul and Mary.

We stood at the top against the railing looking down at the stage and watching the exercisers and families and kids.

On the way back down the stairs I was running up and down each section and still keeping up with George going down... of course he kept stopping to look at me, so he wasn't going very fast.

Some of the railings were rusted clear through.

Next on our agenda was going to another type of tourist attraction. Casa Bonita restaurant in the Denver area has cliff diving entertainment while you dine.

It is very popular among kids, we learned as we pulled into the lot and saw two school buses and about a dozen pre-school buses.

Inside we found the noise of lots of people and kids reverberating off the walls. There was a LONG line. George laughed; he was up for the adventure.

After ordering we stood in line and moved down to where plates of food were coming off a conveyor belt. Two women were looking at tickets and setting the right plate on your tray.

430

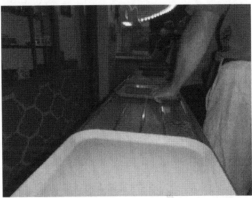

I don't know the seating capacity of the place, but there were rooms with tables in every direction. Each room has a different decorative theme.

We were right near the pond where the divers performed every 15 minutes. Sometimes there was a skit before the person fell into the water. The kids watched, chased and screamed...

I went to the restroom and when I returned to the table, George says, "Ahh, you got something on your shoe..."

After we were done eating we walked around to see the place. There were so many people we walked in with and yet we walked through at least four rooms that weren't being used.

Still in search of a bike map, I drove us to the Tourist Info Center in Denver.

It is right downtown.

We got a bike map! Now, if the weather ever cools we can go for a bike ride.

By our car I saw a meter away from the curb. It was for raising funds for the homeless.

When we got into the car, the car thermometer said it was 100 degrees outside.

Tomorrow we will stay out of the heat!

Day 74 - I Need My Kool!!!!

I didn't get mad at George. I got mad at my poor management of the situation. But that was all later in the day.

This is how the day started...

Gus the cat likes to dump water down the drain and listen to it drip. So we set a bowl with water in the shower and it keeps him occupied. Some evenings I forget to put the bowl away...

The noise of the bowl rattling around in the master shower greeted us first thing this morning...

Smiles.

We don't answer the owner's house phone. The phone announces who is calling. One person keeps calling and it sounds like the machine is saying, "Call from Pimp. Call from Pimp." Hmmmm....

George chuckles.

George was doing well this morning. He turned his phone on and he had a message there from his friend, Glen.

I called Glen (since George doesn't know how to do that anymore) and George chatted on the phone like old times! He was rubbing his hair as he talked just like he used to do, asking questions and responding sensibly.

I decided that we would ride to the community building and join for the month so we can work out and take classes.

I had a low front tire for the second time in a row. George changed the tire quickly while I watered the flowers.

They have lots of weight machines, cardio machines, and free weights to choose from at the gym.

George was done in half an hour. I had packed a book for him. I guided him to a comfortable chair and I continued my workout. Then I put him through some stretches before we left.

After lunch it was too hot to go back out and play. We cut each other's' hair. Just a little trim, I told George. So he just trimmed the bangs and around the ears. Good enough! Soon I won't be able to use his hair cutting assistance. But for now I take the chance.

Dinner time we had shade on the deck and it had cooled off a few degrees.

I told George that tomorrow we were going to drive to a trail and ride into downtown Denver.

Later I saw the door to the garage was open. George was outside.

"George, you have to keep this door closed. The cat will get out!" I yelled out to him.

I closed the door and went about doing whatever it was I was doing... which I don't remember. I felt it was important stuff, I felt busy, too busy to stop and check on what George was doing....

A few minutes later I saw the door to the garage was open again.

"GEOOORGE! Keep this door shut. The cat will get out!" I yelled out the door before shutting it again. I made a sticky note. "CLOSE THIS DOOR!" and stuck it to the door.

I heard the car horn beep... Then the car door open and close and the car horn beep again.

Then George came in and left the door open.

I quietly closed the door and in a quiet but not so calm voice said, "George, this door has to stay closed. We don't want Gus to get outside. I put this note here to remind you."

Then I asked, "What were you doing outside?"

"I put the bikes in the car," he said and looked so proud.

"Oh good. Thanks! Did you put the bike shoes in there?" I asked.

"Yep," he smiled.

"Helmets and my hat?" I asked.

"Uhhhh, no."

I handed him my hat.

"I can't," he said. "The car is locked."

I went to get the keys and then I remembered the keys were in the trunk of my bike. Then I realized the car beep was the car trying NOT to lock because IT knew the keys were in the car. George must have persisted enough that the car GAVE UP.

I walked around the car and checked all the doors. LOCKED, LOCKED, LOCKED.

George said, "I can't put the helmets in, the car is locked. You need to unlock it."

"What I am trying to tell you George is that my keys are with my trike, inside the car."

I panicked... "SHIT SHIT SHIT! I can't believe this! We just found my keys. NOW they are LOCKED in the car!"

I started to doubt my memory; maybe the keys are not in my trunk, because the car doesn't lock if the keys are in the car. I searched the house again. Nope, they are in the trunk on the trike in the car... the locked car.

"Where are your keys?" I asked George.

"In the trunk on my bike," said George.

Sigh...

"I don't know what to do? What do I do?" I asked. But I knew George had no clue. Though he was doing well this morning and most the day... I mean, he THOUGHT to put the bikes and shoes in the car.

I searched on my iPad, "lock smith, Broomfield" and called what turned out to be some kind of referral service or call service.

She took the information. She said someone would call me.

I went with my phone into the driveway to wait...

Then I remembered... INSURANCE! We have Geico and they have roadside service. Suddenly I wasn't so upset and anxious. I pulled out my insurance card and called the number. They said they would send someone and they would be there in 45 minutes.

I hugged George. "Sorry I got so upset," I said. "I really have to find a better way to carry my keys."

The locksmith arrived when George was inside and it was getting dark. The locksmith wrote down the license and got the ID off the windshield. I had to sign a waiver that he was going to break into my car.

He made it look easy to break into my car. Less than three minutes and the doors were open.

The car alarm went off, and I hustled into the car to get the keys out of the trunk and turn the alarm off.

Hurray! My keys! I did the happy dance.

No charge, thank you, Geico!

Days 75 – 76 Cooler Temps

I had announced to a Meetup group that we were going to bike the Platte River Trail today and would start at 9:00 a.m. We had left the house in plenty of time to get to the trail head and unload.

But I got a call as I was about to pull out. Charles lives in Boulder and rides a trike and somehow saw one of our videos on YouTube and contacted me about going for a ride with him in the Boulder area. How cool is that!??

When I got the call I was excited to connect with a local biker and didn't want to cut it off. We arrived at the trail head five minutes late. I have no idea if anyone else showed up for the ride

The hot days were behind us. It was cool enough this morning to start out with a light jacket.

A few miles from Denver and we passed a huge sewage treatment plant.

But then the smell got worse. Rotting flesh mixed with ammonia from animal urine... A meat ... a cow or pig factory....

My eyes started to water from the strong smells. Twice I gagged.

I fondly remembered our rides earlier this trip when we road past fields of clover and bathed in the sweet pleasant smell. Sometimes we were on trails where there was an occasional hint of jasmine.

We stopped at a kiosk that talked about the people buried in the old cemetery. One woman, Aunt Clara Brown, was a freed slave from Kansas who set up a laundry service for the miners and ended up investing in some mines and making money. She used her money to help free slaves and search for her daughter and husband that had been sold away from her. Some people are SOOO amazing.

We passed one place where the smell of ammonia and blood was very strong. They had wires over the fence. They really REALLY didn't want anyone climbing over the fence.

In the heart of Denver...

We kept riding through town along the river.

The clouds were dissipating, and the sun was out. We stopped by the Humane Society and put on sunscreen.

Someone must have donated a lot of money for a mirror-covered dog in the front yard of the Humane Society.

Back in Denver we found a deli for lunch.

I studied the map. We had been given a list of places to see in Denver. One was the State Capital.

On our way we went under a bridge where a homeless person was covered and sleeping... I suppose.

As I was going up the hill after the underpass, I heard George yell something. I looked back and he had stopped.

I went back. He was only a few feet from the sleeping person. George wasn't going anywhere. His chain was stuck between the spokes and the cassette (gears).

We had a LOT of trouble with this on our bike ride from Northern Illinois to Florida in the summer of 2014. (You can find that journal on www.crazyguyonabike.com, search for Susan Straley.)

I couldn't remember the solution to this problem. I remembered learning the solution... but I couldn't remember what the solution was!

I did remember we still had the screwdriver that we used as a lever. I worked on it for quite some time. Finally I was able to pry the chain free, bit by bit.

I told George, "Don't use low gear now until we get this fixed."

"I won't," he said. And I worried he would forget, or think the problem no longer existed because it didn't happen in a while. That was his thinking on our trip from Illinois... and it happened over and over again.

We locked the trikes to a lamp post outside the Capital and went in.

I didn't know this, but the Colorado Governor refused to intern the Asian Americans during WWII! He stood up against the status quo! Cool.

In one area there is a wall with pictures of all the US Presidents.

What will they do when they run out of room? And the big question of the day is…who will be the next one???

I tried to work our way back to the river and the trail. Every time I thought I had a route it turned out to be a one way.

I wasn't taking a picture of the map here. This woman had a tattoo necklace. George is often saying, "People have a lot of tattoos here." AND "There is a lot of eye candy here."

Eye candy is pretty women with a lot of leg showing.

The cool thing about trying to find your way is you sometimes come across things that surprise and delight.

Like the art museum...

A place for teaching how to stop terrorism...

A big mama cow and her bull calf - The Cattlemen Association is very influential in the Colorado capital.

We got to the Cherry Creek Trail that runs into the Platte River.

We got back on the Platte River Trail and headed back to our van.

A total of 42 miles.

George only ran into me twice. The bracket that holds my back fender is now broken. It is a good thing he no longer drives.

It was after 5:00 when we headed for home. Gus the cat greeted us and rubbed against our legs. He doesn't like to be picked up. We are tempted but he has let us know that he will bite if we try.

After dinner I check email. My friend in Wisconsin, Kathi, contacted me after she saw in this blog that we had visited Arvada. She let me know that we have mutual friends that live in Arvada, CO. Sandy and Steve used to be a part of a very fun weekend bike group we had in Wisconsin.

I was able to get in touch with Sandy, and we have arranged to meet for breakfast on the 15th!

Day 76 was a good day of taking care of business and just hanging out... with Gus the cat.

ALZHEIMER'S TRIPPIN' with George

I looked at the class schedule at the community center and I decided we would try the Silver Sneakers and the yoga classes which run back-to-back on Fridays.

The Silver Sneakers class was more like an aerobic dance class. And though the moves were simple, George really had a hard time copying what the instructor was doing. I kept catching his eye in the mirror and smiling real big like we were having a great time and he would smile back. He didn't complain at all.

After class the instructor came over, and I told her that George has dementia and he did pretty well. She gave him lots of praise and encouragement. It really helps the brain to try moving differently, she told him. Keep doing it!

Yoga class was more flow and not holding poses. I enjoyed the class. The instructor came over and tried to correct George once, and I winced inside. I don't think it bothered him; I hope not. We will see if I get him back in a Silver Sneakers or a yoga class next week.

Back at home I made some green beans and rice with slivered almonds... I spilled some of the slivered almonds.

After lunch I had George get out the vacuum and clean them up. He did pretty well. I only had to go over a little of it again.

Many wives do this when their husbands don't have dementia. I have never had to. George has always been methodical and thorough. Now, I have to remind him to shower and change his underwear. And sometimes when he does a task, I have to finish it for him.

I started exploring our options for after we leave Broomfield. I have mixed feelings. I got an email from the people of the Airbnb we just left in Boulder. They had washed the sheets and found they were stained where the arms and back would be. I knew right away it was from the sun guard that George puts on when we are doing outside activities. They wanted to know how to get the stains out.

I don't have a clue. I stopped using white shirts and sheets long ago. Even then there is a film I can't get out. I suggested Dawn and water.

I had my computer upstairs in the spare bedroom. I found a TV tray and set myself up in the living room so the three of us could hang out together.

In the early evening we went for a walk in the neighborhood.

These are brilliant fire-cracker looking flowers. I don't know what they are, but they are pretty...

Back home we had popcorn and watched a movie on Netflix.

Tomorrow afternoon I have let the Meetup group know we are going to the Leftapalooza in Longmont. It is a tribute band contest and starts at noon. They said they will have a flag...

Days 77 – 78 Connecting with Locals

Last night I got a call from Chas in Boulder. He is the guy who saw a video I had created and learned somehow that we ride trikes and are in the area. So he contacted me through YouTube and then via phone and invited us to ride with him.

He has recruited some other trike riders and asked us to meet him on Sunday up by Fort Collins and we would ride the Poudre River Trail together.

Cool!

It suddenly became a priority today to get our trikes fixed.

I set my sights on Rocky Mountain Recumbents in Fort Collins.

The store clerk/owner had us bring George's trike to the back entrance so they could work on it. There was a group of trikers there!

It is a group ride, they told me.

In the blue is Dustin. In the orange helmet is Rustin...

Not brothers, just friends... both with beards, both active in B-Bold -- "Empowered Adaptive Living".

The problem with the stuck chain wasn't the shifter, but the chain was too long. They shortened George's chain and changed a tube on his front tire which was flat when we pulled it out of the van.

They found a part to fix the fender attachment and gave it to George.

The charge was $51 for the repairs and parts.

We left the shop and drove toward Longmont where Leftapalooza was going on.

We stopped at Batteries Plus and got George a new battery for his car fob. He was happy. I was nervous. I reminded him to be careful.

We arrived at the concert. The event is hosted by Left Hand Brewery (Hence the name). We found the flag indicating the Longmont Social Club... only no one around the flag knew anything about the Longmont Social Club.

Later, two people sat in the green chairs and I asked them. Yes! They were it.

I didn't like the music. In the middle of some punk band tribute, I said, I have had enough.

452

Tomorrow we ride with new friends! YEAHHHHH!!

Day 78 and I am excited! We were meeting up with local trike riders today to ride a part of the Poudre River Trail in Fort Collins.
We arrived about ten minutes early. No one else was there yet.

Then Esmaa and William arrived. We have company!

They own an organic farm outside of Loveland. They just started riding trikes this year. They used to be heavy hikers, but their joints were feeling some wear. So they switched to trikes. They are tackling the trike riding like they have done their hiking. They ride 60 miles three times a week, going as fast as they can.

Today they were going to take it easy for us, and I was glad of that.

Then Chas and Sharon showed up. Thanks for reaching out and being persistent, Chas!

There were lots of sunny areas, but stretches of cottonwood trees near the river provided shade on the trail.

453

There was a diamond frame biker in front of us hauling his son in a recumbent style kid-tandem or third wheel thing. The kid yelled "HIIII" every time we passed them or they passed us. Just before we stopped to take this picture, they were in front of us. One of their tires when Poooooshhhhhh. "Uh- oh...."

We offered to help, but the man said their car was close by. He took our picture. Asmaa said she would miss the little boy and his cheerful greetings.

We arrived at a little town at the end of the trail, our turnaround point.

We got back to the cars after 4:00 p.m. after 46 miles.

We all said we would ride together again before George and I left the area. They were a nice group to ride with, staying together and upbeat.

After dinner as I was cleaning up. I went to use the garbage disposal, and the button was pushed in all the way and stuck in that position.

I asked George if he knew what happened.

"I pushed it," he said.

"Did the garbage disposal turn on when you pushed it?" I asked.

He shook his head.

"I will have to call the repair man, and we will pay for it," I said.

While I was uploading pictures and checking and responding to emails, Gus the cat kept me company... but not too close.

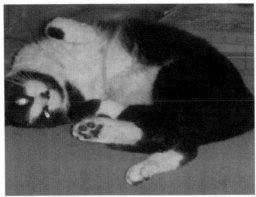

Tomorrow I have repair people to call, book work and stuff... just stuff like cooking and groceries and research for voting in our local school board election.

George will read and surf on his iPad (I hope).

Days 79 – 80 Repair and Maintenance

At breakfast George asked me what we were going to do today.

I said I had stuff to do and we would hang out here and maybe later we would go to the gym.

We have been here a week. So it is time to do laundry.

Mary Ann, a bike friend from Florida had suggested Pinesol for removing stains from clothes and sheets. I was afraid that George's sun screen soaked arms and legs might have also stained the sheets here. I also mixed water and dawn and got the pillow cases wet with it.

YEAH! No stains.

While I was doing laundry and emptying the dishwasher and calling the repair guys...George read and surfed. Then I saw him standing with the Windex in hand.

"What are you doing?" I asked.

He was silent. I asked if he was going to wash the windows in the car.

"Yes," he said.

I found him a rag that would work, and I moved the car into the shade. He cleaned the windows.

Which was a good thing! I don't have to worry what he is doing.

I called the repair guy about the garbage disposal. He said he would come by around 5:00 p.m. I asked him about fixing the sprinkler and he gave me the name of the guy that works on Dick's sprinkler system.

I called that guy and arranged for him to come after 4:30 too.

I answered email and did bookkeeping work that I have been neglecting.

I chopped up a leek and sweet potato and regular potatoes that Arlene had asked us to use up while they were gone. I used ginger and cinnamon for seasoning with veggie broth. It turned out pretty yummy!

We got a call from our son Jeremy. I turned the phone over to George and George thought to ask after Jeremy's wife, but couldn't remember her name.

We go to the gym at 3:00 p.m.

At the store I also bought a new thermos. My coffee thermos had broken. I picked out a pretty teal one.

As we were pulling out of the grocery store I saw it was 4:30! Oh my! I might miss the sprinkler guy.

I pulled in the drive just as the sprinkler guy was about to leave.

The sprinkler is fixed.

When I got in the house, George was putting ice in the teal thermos I had bought. "I thought I bought it for my coffee," I said.

George didn't say anything. He just kept filling the thermos with ice and water. I remembered that he had shown me the hinge on his water thermos had busted when the thermos was dropped the other day.

"If I had known the thermos was for you I would have gotten you and orange or a black one," I said. George just looked at me and smiled.

I looked at him...

He drank from the thermos...

"You like the teal one?" I ask.

He nods and smiles.

"OK then! The teal one is yours!"

Derrel arrived to fix the garbage disposal.

"The problem is you pushed it all the way in. Just tap it a bit and it will start. Then tap it again and it will stop," Derrel explained when he was done.

I told George, "Just tap it."

George looked a bit foggy.

Re-thinking it I say, "I will do the garbage disposal from now on."

As Derrel left I asked how much and he said we didn't have to pay, it was Dick's house.

I said, "We broke it. So I feel we should pay for the repair."

He thought a moment and said, "Twenty bucks." Nice!

In the evening I found the hand trowel and I went out and dug dandelions and trimmed the rose bushes... it is called "dead-heading." Trim off the flowers as they wilt so that the energy of the plant goes into making more flowers instead of making seeds.

Pulling weeds is so satisfying, especially when you get the whole root.

Rise and shine! Ding ding ding! It's the **80th day** of our journey.

Coffee and the newspaper make me happy.

Coffee and the newspaper make me high.

John Denver I am not.

What's happening right now while we travel, besides the Presidential campaigns and the strong opinions on both sides of the aisle? The Olympics in Rio is happening.

I said we would go for a bike ride. George went out and took the trikes out of the car.

I gathered up stuff and went outside. Then I thought that George probably didn't change his incontinence pad this morning, which means he might overflow. I ran upstairs and got a pad and a change of underwear and shorts for him. I rolled them up and I will keep them on my bike for an emergency. I feel at that moment like a competent caregiver.

I had mapped a route to Erie to a restaurant with Carrot in the name. I figured if it had carrot in the name, it must offer some vegetarian options.

We came to a park that had informational signs on the history of the area. It was mind boggling. If they laid out the history of the earth (or maybe life on earth) such that one foot equals a million years. Human existence would take up about one half inch.

We came across a vacant city lot that was full of prairie dogs. I was so focused on getting a picture that....

I rode right into a large crack in the pavement.

George followed me.

No damage done, we continued.

We rode through a neighborhood with new construction and big houses.

The trail I had mapped out to get to Erie was mostly cement, with areas of packed gravel.

Steep hills and loose gravel are impossible to climb on a trike. The back wheel just spins like on ice.

I locked my brakes, got off my trike, and pushed George up the hill before walking my trike up.

I loved it! I turned around with a big smile.
"You having fun?" I asked George.
"No," he said.

"No? What's wrong?"

"It's too hard," George said.

I checked to see if his brakes were stuck on. No, that wasn't the problem.

"You want an apple?" I asked.

George ate his apple, and we rested and watched the construction workers just down the road working on a new house.

There are very few signs showing us which way. I had to stop a lot and consult the iPad.

When we arrived in Erie.it was getting hot. I was looking forward to some cold water in the shade.

I asked George, "Are you having fun yet?"

"No," he said.

I looked at him waiting for him to elaborate. Stomach? Head? Tired? He saw the concern in my face and changed his answer, "Yes."

"You're OK? You're feeling better?" I asked.

"Yes," he said.

I have no way of knowing if he understands the question, if he is feeling poorly, if I should be concerned.

I planned to head back starting on the Coal Creek Trail.

There was absolutely NO shade. The sun got hotter and hotter...

I stopped under a bridge and re-applied sun screen. I refilled our waters from the extra thermos. I poured a little water on the scarf I wore around my neck.

Did I tell you the sun was merciless? We passed some solar panels and I thought this would be a good place for LOTS of solar collectors.

NO SHADE and it is HOT and dry. My stomach is full of water, my mouth is dry.

I said, "We are bakin'... bacon... sizzling like bacon..."

A TREE!!!!! YEAH!!! A TREE!!! Thank you tree!!!

We sat and drank and enjoyed the breezes. I checked my email and got good news from our friends, Mark and Jane. They just became grandparents. Smiles...

We got back on the trail and into the heat.

I ran out of water and there was nothing around in view. We finally came to a medical center. We went in there to refill our waters. Then back in the heat, we started to climb.

I tried to take a picture of the switchbacks to show how much we rode up hill on gravel.

Boy! Were we glad to get home! Right away I poured some Kombucha for George and me and cut up a cold muskmelon.

George refilled his glass. He drank the whole bottle of Kombucha!
I had a few slices of melon. George ate the rest of the whole melon!
I pulled out the chips and salsa to replace our salt.
The clouds came over, the wind picked up, a few rain drops fell.

George finished the book, <u>Pretty Little Lies</u>. He took a shower. He smells good now.

Me too...

I got a reply from one of my Affordable Travel Club inquiries. We have a place to stay for a couple nights at the end of August near Zion National Park in Utah. The host reminded me it would be HOT there. Ohhhh... ya that's right...

Day 81 – 82 Rainy Day House Sitter Blues

I had planned to have a day to just hang out. Go to the gym, research opportunities and travel routes for after we leave Denver. That was the plan...

In the morning we rode to the gym. We did weight-lifting and then the Cardio-Silver Sneakers class. It's fun.

I am feeling fortunate.

Back at home I made soup adding some ingredients to the potato soup I had made the other day. While it was cooking, I pulled out some maps and tour books and tried to make some decisions about where to go next.

I was thinking we would drive to Dillon tomorrow and ride the trail up to Frisco and Breckenridge where Charlie of Boulder told us was a trail we should not miss.

George asked, "What are we doing today?"

I told him, "We will just stay close, hang out, get things done, plan some of the rest of our trip..."

Later he asked again.

I explained again.

Then he asked again, and I said, "You want to do something?"

He nodded. I was frustrated.

Now instead of doing what I NEEDED to do I had to figure out something interesting to do TODAY. It was supposed to be hot today -- hiking and biking were off list.

After some research and thought, I gave him three options of things to do.

Three options were probably too much for him to process at this stage of his dementia. As a person loses cognition the options need to be simpler. Eventually, I will be making all the decisions and he may or may not notice.

This time I gave him three options:

He chose the Nature Preserve.

After soup, I started to get ready. At one point I walked outside to do something in the backyard. I walked out the garage which is the door that the owners prefer we use. There is a people door from the house to the garage and an overhead door for the cars to get in and out. So we have to use the electric door opener to open the overhead door every time we want to leave the house.

I went outside to get something off the bikes.

A half a minute later George was out there too, following me around.

When I returned to the garage through the overhead door, there was Gus the cat in the garage!

Fortunately, when I yelled, "GEORGE!" the cat ran back through the open pedestrian door to the house.

I said to George in a loud voice, "George you HAVE to keep this door to the house SHUT or the cat will get out!"

And George was right behind me and said, "It's no problem."

"YES IT IS!!! We are supposed to be taking care of this cat! We don't want the cat to get out!"

George was NEVER one to leave doors and cabinets and drawers open. He sometimes drove me nuts following me around and closing things I had deliberately left open because I was going back into that room, cabinet, drawer in just a bit. Sometimes I left it open because my hands would be full or covered in goo or something.

Now, even with a note on the door, George follows me around and doesn't close the door.

Sigh. I didn't feel guilty about yelling. I know it isn't his fault. That part of his brain is fading. But I am hoping that my anger might impress another part of his brain to close the door.... we will see.

All packed up we head out.

The Arsenal Nature Preserve had a watering tank out in the field and a buffalo was there.

As I suspected, the Arsenal was used during the World War to make weapons... chemical weapons. And they made this bomb proof phone....

473

Uhh... didn't they use telephone lines back then? Wouldn't a bomb destroy the lines???

We took the car around an auto route in the preserve. We saw a deer and watched it for a while. Then as more cars stopped to look and people got out to take pictures it bounced off. Boing boing boing...

George and I found some shade from a bush and stood watching a buffalo approach.

I drove us toward a movie theater close by.

The shopping area where the multiplex theater is located has narrow streets that are pedestrian friendly. Shop after shop after shop....

We walked from the parking past three blocks of up-scale and mid-scale shops. There were bigger stores around like Macys and Big Bass Pro and a Target Super store.

We looked at the movies. The only one I would watch, "Nine Lives," wasn't showing for an hour and 40 minutes.

We got a slice of pizza, walked over to Target and looked at watches and a replacement thermos for George.

The movie was ... silly and the constant irritating noises of the cat were obnoxious. We were glad when the movie ended.

Back at home we discovered one of the slats on the blinds had come off. Probably Gus was trying to look outside. We shouldn't close the blinds.

The blind was busted at the top. I will have to figure out a fix for it.

We were both tired. I wondered if we would have the energy for a drive to Dillon and ride up the mountain tomorrow. It is supposed to be a bit cooler...

Day 82 started with another dose of pancakes.

Over breakfast I asked George if he was up to biking up in the mountains today. He said he wasn't and I was kind of glad, because I was tired too and felt like I needed to stay in one place and rest.

George was watching machines on YouTube. His entire career he worked designing and improving manufacturing machines. They still fascinate him.

I responded to email. A tenant had abandoned the only property we still own. They left it a mess. Though I paid for pest control for several years, the people that came in to clean and paint found a roach infestation.

I had to deal with that.

When I checked the clock is was after noon already!

After lunch I heard water running. Dick had told me that the water softener runs in the afternoon. But a while later it was still running, and I thought I better investigate to make sure it was the softener.

Here is what I found. I heard spraying water coming from where the main water supply comes in through the basement cement wall before it reaches the water meter.

I could not see the water gauge so I pulled up a chair and stood on the chair to see. The gauge was not moving. That means the leak was happening on its way into the house.

But still, I tried turning off levers.

Fortunately the amount coming into the house was minimal and had not caused damage to the stacks of boxes and stuff in the basement.

I went outside and tried to find a main shut-off. I found one valve and turned it to off. But still the water kept coming.

There were several boxes in the yard that said main valve. But when I went into them is was just wires. No shut-off valve.

I called Dick's son and left a message, I called Derrel the repair guy and Glen the sprinkler guy. They both said call the plumber. I called the plumber and they said they won't do anything without talking to the owner of the property.

I walked the parameter of the property looking for the city water input valve. I couldn't find one.

The whole time I am going up and down the stairs and around the yard, George is a few steps behind me. It is like there is an elastic string that attaches him to me. I had pulled out a screw driver and other tools from the garage to help me get off the lids of the boxes in the yard. He started to put them away. "I may not be done," I said. "Leave them please."

There was a pile of leaves outside above where the leak was happening in the basement. The ground out from the house was soggy and spongey.

I called the water department and told them that I thought it was an issue between the gauge and the city water supply. They sent someone out pretty prompt. It took him about 20 minutes to find the valve and turn it off. It was buried under sod. He had to use a metal detector and then poke at it with a rod to see if the size of the object was the size of the box he sought.

While the city guy worked, I sat in the shade and did some yoga stretches, working at remaining calm.

He turned the water off. It stopped the leaking. Now there is no water to the house. I try calling the owners and they are having their calls forwarded to Arlene's office assistant. She suggested I send them an email.

I checked the time on the world clock on the iPad. It was 11 p.m. in Paris. I sent them an email and gave them the phone number and website for the plumber.

We had to go get some water for drinking and washing. I went to Walgreens first and we found a thermos like George's old thermos and some dark-chocolate mint M&M's. Smiles!

We then went to a large grocery store across the street from Walgreens where we got water.

Gus had disappeared when the Water Department guy was in the house. I was glad to see him come out to greet us when we got home.

I searched and found a supply of paper plates and cups that we could use in the interim. I told George we would use the water to flush only when it was brown.

We belong to the community rec center, we can shower there. It's all good.

After dinner we went for a walk and did our exercises.

We then walked to a bench, and we watched the city lights come on.

While we sat there, I proposed three options for after we leave here on the 23rd. George did not give any response. No help in making that decision.

We sat on the bench together and waited for the dark. There was supposed to be a meteor shower tonight. I put my head on George's shoulder. We both started yawning. We began walking home before it got dark enough to see the stars.

Day 83 – 85 Without Running Water

I didn't want to make a mess in the kitchen that I couldn't clean up without access to running water. I used that as an excuse to go out to breakfast.

Sometime during the morning I took a picture of my phone so I would remember I got a call... or I made a call... Anyway I don't remember the call now...

Maybe it was the owner's office personnel letting me know that they have arranged for a plumber to fix the pipe. Only thing is, it is Friday and the plumber has to pull a permit. Therefore, he will not be able to work on the pipe until MONDAY.

We will be the whole weekend without running water.

No big deal. We have water. We will just clean up on Monday once the water is running, I say. Thankfully we have memberships at the Rec Center and can shower there.

I had bought tickets to a dance concert for tonight. I packed each of us a set of clean clothes and the basic toiletries we would need so we could shower before we went to the concert.

I got a call from the owner's son. He was going to call another plumber and try to get them out to the house to give another quote. The owner emailed and said the first plumber quoted $3,500, but it may go higher once they get down in and see what needs to be done.

We stuck around all afternoon. The son never called back, we never got a call or a visit from a plumber. I used some of our precious water to water some of the thirsty flowers in the back yard.

At 4 p.m. we gathered our stuff and went to the Rec Center for our shower. The water is on a one-minute timer and you can't adjust the temperature. Fortunately you can re-push the button when it starts to get to the end of the minute and get another minute.

I had not remembered to pre-arrange a meeting place after our showers. I was waiting downstairs and George was waiting upstairs. After about ten minutes I decided to look around and there he was, sitting in a comfortable chair doing nothing but waiting.

It was only 5:00 and the dance performance wasn't until 7:00. We drove over to find the theater.

We were right next to a park with some statues and a pond.

There was a 9/11 memorial. It was nicely done with a stone and artwork for all three locations that were hit on 9/11. The twin towers, the Pentagon, and the plane that the passengers took down to keep the plane from being used to crash into something.

I don't recall ever seeing a timeline laid out of the events of the day. George blew his nose... I felt choked-up too.

As the United States and the World attempted to make sense of the day's events, recovery and rescue efforts continued. As hours turned into days and then weeks, a final count was determined showing the magnitude of lives forever lost at all three locations.

The Pentagon & Flight 93 Washington & Shanksville		The World Trade Center New York City	
Total Deaths All 9/11 Attacks	3,030	Total Deaths WTC 9/11 Attack	2,752
Total Injured All 9/11 Attacks	2,337	Total Injured WTC 9/11 Attack	2,261
Total Deaths 9/11 Attack The Pentagon (Ground)	124	Firefighter Deaths WTC 9/11 Attack	343
Total Injured 9/11 Attack The Pentagon	76	Police Deaths WTC 9/11 Attack	75
American Airlines Flight 77 The Pentagon	64	American Airlines Flight 11 WTC North Tower	92
United Airlines Flight 93 Shanksville, PA	40	United Airlines Flight 175 WTC South Tower	65

Back at the theater we found a bench in the shade.
Next to a sculpture...

George laughed when I got down close and took a picture of one of the figures' behind. I defended my action... the pocket is labeled...

At 6:30 the theater doors opened.

It was sad. It was the first performance of this dance company and there were less than 30 people in the audience.

The producer announced before the performance that if we wanted to come back tomorrow night and bring a friend we would get Buy One Get One Free (BOGO).

It was clear that an incredible amount of work went into creating this show.

The main dancer danced every scene and never lost the power and balance of her moves.

On **Day 84** we got to rock to Reggae in Dillon, Colorado.

I planned for us to go to Dillon and ride the trail to Breckenridge.

Because the water is shut off, I have instructed George that we will use only one toilet. We have only had to use it for "number 1," fortunately. Still, it was starting to stink so I poured about one quarter cup of Pine-sol into the toilet bowl yesterday.

This morning I tried pouring two gallons of water into the bowl in hopes it would force it to flush. It didn't.

You never realize how much you use something until you can no longer use it. When you break a bone or sprain a thumb you realize how much you depend on that appendage to open a door, tie your shoe, wipe your bottom, feed yourself.

Cooking, I am constantly rinsing off my hands. Brushing our teeth takes planning ahead for the rinse.

This morning I made us our breakfast. The dishwasher is now full.

"Shall I run it?" George asks.... silence as I just look at him... "Oh yeah, I can't."

The bottom of the sink is covered in crumbs... I don't want to waste the water to wash them down the drain...

I pack an apple and nuts and the two Cliff Bars that I bought in anticipation of this ride today. The trikes are already in the car.

I feed Gus the cat an extra handful of food and scoop out his soiled litter. I know we will be gone until late.

It is at least an hour and a half drive to get to Dillon. We start climbing into the mountains

At a wayside in St. George I learn about a scenic pass that heads south from St. George. I got a map just in case.

We get back on Interstate 70 and as we are coming down a long incline toward Dillon two semi's one in front of us, one behind us, start to smoke. I was worried. I think they both made it without blowing a tire.

In Dillon, I parked by an amphitheater. It looked like they were set up for a walk/run or bike event. I asked and learned the band was starting at 11:00 a.m.

We will miss the band. It was after 10:00 a.m., and we hadn't even started our ride yet.

The intersecting trails are well marked. We are heading to Breckenridge. It is a ski town; we expect it will be mostly uphill.

As we are going into Frisco I think that it would be nice to be here for a few days... maybe after we leave Broomfield, we will come back to the Frisco/Dillon/Breckenridge area.

Sometimes the flowers along the trail were so awesome. I would stop and go back to take pictures... But I could never capture the beauty with a picture.

We enter Breckenridge.

There is a Rec Center with a huge skate park. We stopped to watch the athletes take to the air.

Then I was too hungry to look around much.

We found "EXTREME PIZZA" on Main Street. George still knows how to lock up the bikes and remembers the combination.

The one museum I definitely wanted to visit was the Barney Ford museum. I had read about it in the tourist book. The man was amazing. A slave all his life, he escaped through the Underground Railroad.

He came to Colorado and became quite a businessman. He had learned to read and write because his mother always had the hope that he would someday be free. His mother risked her life to get hold of materials so that he could learn to read.

Barney invested in gold mines and restaurants. He worked for the right for all men to be able to vote as Colorado sought statehood after the Civil War.

The volunteer at the museum had a lot of enthusiasm. She said that a lot of bad things happened to Barney during his lifetime (several of his businesses burned down, some failed) but he just kept going and trying again.

On our way back to Dillon it started to sprinkle and cool off. George and I put on our light jackets.

As we approached Dillon, we could hear music. Was the band still playing?

What we heard was pretty good. Just after we arrived the band members left leaving the drums and sound equipment behind...

I asked someone and he said a Reggae band was going to play, and they were very good. They would be starting at 7:00. He said that was who was playing just now, that it was their sound check.

We stayed. As the sun got lower in the sky it got cooler.

We strolled a couple blocks and I got George a coffee to warm himself. We passed a thrift store! I got two nice jackets for $14

The band, Pato Banton & the Now Generation, did a good job. George and I were swaying and smiling.

Pato was also preaching about love and peace. We all were giving peace signs, rubbing our hearts to gather the love and giving strangers a high-five to pass the love on.

He said, "Love is the most important thing."

George said, "He's got that right!" and he put his arm around me....

Ah sweet! My heart swells.

When we got home I was still wired. George went right to bed.

We were all gooey with sun screen and sweat. I planned the morning. How we would need to shower, but first we would get dressed and have breakfast and pack up a bag to take to the Rec Center...

The bathroom with our designated toilet smelled so strong, the odor floated down the hall and reached us in our bed. It was mostly ammonia and Pine-sol. It didn't bother George.

People all over the world live in areas without sewers, without running water. I remind myself how good we have it, how lucky I am.

I turned on the bathroom fan and closed the bathroom door... but not all the way. I leave the light on in the bathroom and the door open, so we can find our way down the hall in the dark of the night.

After tossing and turning a while, I went downstairs and uploaded pictures onto my laptop computer. I drank chamomile tea. Gus let me pet him.

It was 3:00 a.m. when I returned to bed and relaxed into sleep.

Day 85 we get up in the morning with the sound of Gus rolling his bowl around the shower. He wants to play with water... but there is none.

I get up and make a breakfast of smoothies. I am determined to get enough water to flush the toilet and clean the sinks... which are getting kind of yucky.

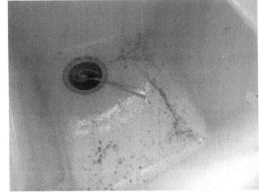

After the breakfast we pack up our clothes. George packs his own bag with clothes, clean incontinence pads, and toiletries without any coaching from me!

I put all the water bottles in the car for filling.

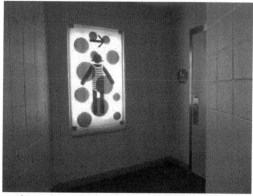

The Rec Center is a nice place to go to shower and work out. George doesn't want to work out after our showers. I do a few Pilates moves. I don't fill the waters at the club because there is not a good flowing spigot. It would take forever to get eight gallons of water from a drinking fountain or low-flow shower head.

Let's go do laundry! There we can fill our waters in the wash tub at the laundromat.

While we sat there, I had my Kindle book. George had nothing to read. I asked him if he would like me to read to him. He said, "I don't care."

I started filling him in on where I was in the story and then started reading. At one point I heard him say, "Uh huh," like he would if I was talking to him and he was ... pretending to listen.

I couldn't believe it. It was 11:30 by the time we were done with laundry! Half the day was gone, and all we did was shower and do one load of laundry.

Yeah! Water enough to clean the sink a bit and do a few dishes.

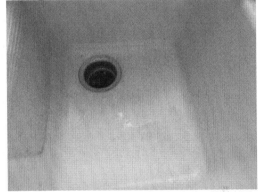

It takes four full gallons of water to flush the toilet. That is two trips up the stairs carrying a full gallon in each hand. Not that that is hard work... but it sure isn't an efficient way to deal with human waste. If we all had to haul water to flush our waste we would come up with a more efficient system.

An odorless composting system or something... a hole in the ground....

Later in the afternoon there was shade in the yard. I pulled out our yoga mats and led George through some yoga poses. His hamstrings and hips are very tight. His hands no longer bend back to 90 degrees from his fore-arm.

"I should stretch him more often. Several times a day," I think.

Then another part of my mind protests that I do enough, and I am NOT a nurse-maid...

How much care to give? It is a constant battle in my head and heart.

Later we sat in the shade and ate ice cream.

497

While we were sitting there, I noticed some of the plants were thirsty. I went next door and knocked. They were home! I told them we were without water and asked if I could get some from their hose. "Sure!" he said. He helped me fill some jugs and then showed me where he had an outdoor spigot where I could hook up a hose.

Yeah! Close access to water. I watered the plants and even dumped some on areas of the yard that were turning brown already.

At around 7:00 p.m. we took a walk.

Tomorrow the plumbers come. I had to postpone our breakfast meeting with our Wisconsin bike friends who live now in Arvada, Colorado. We will have to stay home and wait for the plumbers to complete their work.

If we get running water, man, I am going to clean!

Day 86 - Plumbers and Tears and Shit -- Oh My!

August 15, 2016, the day the plumbers are supposed to arrive. We are both hoping they will be able to fix the problem in one day. If they do, we will have clean water to wash with and cook with and flush with.

We can't leave the house. We have to wait around for the plumbers to arrive. No one has told us when they might arrive.

After breakfast, while I am cleaning up the kitchen, George informs me he has to "take a crap." I tell him to use the designated toilet. Then I tell him to get four gallons of water and put all four gallons of water in the tank and then flush.

We now have a hose hooked up to the neighbor's outdoor spigot. So we can get some water, fill the toilet tank and flush.

George fills up the gallons, goes upstairs. I hear the toilet flush. Then he comes back downstairs and starts filling gallons again. I come outside to check on him.

"It didn't go down?" I ask.

"Not all of it," he said.

"Did you use four gallons?" I ask.

"No... three," he says.

So I help him fill four and go upstairs with him.

It is a little floater. No big problem. After all four gallons are in George flushes and the persistent little bugger is still floating.

"Don't worry about it. We'll flush when the plumbing is working again," I say.

As we descend the stairs. The plumber appears at the front door. YEAH!

They come in, look at the problem and listen to what I observed. The lead plumber says they will have to dig down and replace the pipe through the wall and out to the street. But they cannot start until the utilities come out and mark where the wires are so they don't break any wires.

In the meantime, they start covering the floors to protect them from the dust and dirt. I thought that was very respectful and professional.

Gus is nervous to have strangers in the house.

George goes to work watching "Bones" on his iPad.

The owner is emailing me, "Are they there? Can you take another picture of the area where the pipe is; we can't figure out where it is from the pictures you sent before."

I get ready to take some pictures but no I have to go number two.

No problem. We have access to water. I can fill the tank and flush.

I go, I fill the tank, I flush and "OH SHIT!!!"

The toilet is overflowing!

Fortunately Dick keeps a plunger right by the toilet and with a little careful plunging, so as not to spill too much... I am able to clear the drain.

Then I fill four more gallons and flush again.

In the meantime the plumbers have started working...

I like this plumber. He is smart enough to wear waist-high undies. No ugly plumber's crack!

I take a picture of the corner of the basement where one of the plumbers is drilling a hole in the cement.

Yes, as I told you, the owners like lots of stuff...

I upload the pictures to the owner. I look up and George just finished his second episode of "Bones" and he is teary.

"You are emotional today," I say.

He nods. I go over and hug him and he cries a little.

"Did Bones have an emotional story this time?" I asked.

"Yes," he says as he sheds a few tears on my shoulder. This sensitivity is a new characteristic for him. I have always been the one blowing my nose after a show. He would chuckle and hug me.

The plumbers have the thing almost fixed and then the city water valve busts.

When the CITY water valve breaks there is no easy way to turn off the flow... Now they have mud in their ditch.

He told me they use dry ice to create an ice dam in the pipe until they could get a new valve on. They must keep some on hand for jobs like this...

He showed me the pipe that came out of the cement wall. It was damaged by knocking against the cement wall when the water is turned on and off.

While they were working, I repaired one of the jackets that I bought at the thrift store in Dillon, on Saturday. I had seen the damage before I bought. But I liked the color and it fit and all the damage was on the seams.

I had bought a sewing kit for $1.00 the other day to sew a button back on George's pants. I made use of that kit. It even had two kinds of pink thread!

The plumber came and said they were all done, but they had to wait for the city inspector to come before they could close things up. He showed me that they put a plastic tube around the pipe where it goes through the wall so it won't rub against the cement when it moves slightly.

It was after noon now. The plumbers took their lunch break while they are waiting for the replacement part for the busted city valve.

Gus came out from hiding and was rubbing against our legs.

Later the plumber said the new part was in, the inspector approved, and they were able to finish up.

All cleaned up. They left and Gus was really happy to be out with us again.

We have WATER!!! I ran the dish washer. I went out and moved a sprinkler around to areas of the yard that had started turning brown without the sprinkler system working.

I cleaned the kitchen sink and ran the garbage disposal.

I took more pictures and sent them to the owners.

At one point I looked up and George was watching another BONES! I think he watched four episodes today.

I knew it was time to get some better books for George and me.

We took a road trip to the book store.

It used to be that when we went to the book store, George would go to the non-fiction business section. Now at the book store or the library he just follows me around. He has no clue of what to look for.

I asked him if he enjoyed the last book. He said he did. I found one by the same author. We got two books.

After supper, George started reading one of the books.

After a day of sitting around, we are ready. Tomorrow we ride.

Days 87 – 88 Triking and Business

Only four days to our 40th wedding anniversary!

Today we ride. I wrote down the turn-by-turn instructions so we won't have to stop and look at google maps as often.

It is wonderful to walk into a bathroom that smells like face soap and fresh towels!

Leaving the house, I couldn't get the security system to turn on. It said it wasn't ready, which means a door is open.

I went around and re-closed and locked all the doors. Still not ready... Then I remembered one of the plumbers asked about opening a basement window. I went down and checked... it looked closed... I put my hand against it and felt screen, not window. Once the window was closed the security system worked fine.

In the meantime George is waiting in the driveway ready to roll.

The trail was paved and the signs guiding the way were well-designed and placed so we could see them.

We had very few traffic crossings.

Soon we could see the Flatirons near Boulder.

Lots of sunflowers and YES! Bees!

We climbed quite a bit and came to a scenic overlook.

We arrived in Boulder. I had my sights on dining at a vegetarian restaurant near Pearl Street in downtown Boulder.

We sat outside. The thing is, we used to talk. We would talk about the business George ran, we would talk about our friends, and we would talk about our vacation plans or what we need to do investing or with the house.

Now... we just sit. Sometimes he says, "I love you." and I say it back.

Sometimes I chat and when I ask questions, he makes answers that sometimes make sense and sometimes don't. I am grateful for the silence, sometimes. There are no long stressful talks, when we disagree about what to do with our time and money.

The lunch is great. I get a falafel burger, and it is crispy and moist (which means greasy, but I don't care).

We headed back to the Bear Creek Trail to get to the Foothills Trail that will take us to the Hwy 36 Trail. All these trail choices is pretty cool!

But then again, sometimes you can end up here...

Presto - we are on the 36 Trail. Pavement... no shade and now we are biking back up up up out of the valley.

I stopped to drink and rest and let George catch up three times on that hill. And then we were at the scenic overlook and the brochure display created some shade. We spent about fifteen minutes there cooling off.

513

When we got back, I said we are going to do your exercises and stretch right away or we won't do it.

I asked George if he had to use the bathroom first.

"No," he said and shook his head.

We go into the back yard in the shade and we do one stretch and breath deep six times and then he says, "I got to take a crap."

"OK," I say and I watch him have to hang onto the wall of the house as he walks, he's a bit unsteady on his feet. We need the stretching.

We shower for the second time that day. It is nice to have access to running water and a shower.

I remember today is the day we are to pick up our mail. I tell George I am going to the Post Office and of course, he wants to go along.

Good things were in the mail! Checks and no bills... well, one bill.

From the pest control company I have been paying to treat the house we own in Huntsville, Alabama. You know, the house that we just found out was INFESTED WITH ROACHES!!! Yes, that company had sent us a bill.

Guess what, I am not paying it. Obviously they have been billing us and not ENTERING the property! In fact this bill says that the treatment occurred after the tenant moved out.

Breathe, Sue. Just breathe and let it go. It's evening. I cook rice and bok choy and we chill.

Day 88 we plan to stick close to home. We have an hour before the Rec Center has Silver Sneakers followed by a Pilate's class. George has never done Pilates... he says he will do it.

Over breakfast I browse the paper. Ford has announced that in five years they will have "driverless" cars without steering and pedals.

After breakfast we go the Rec Center for the Pilates Class..

We got out our mats and the instructor gave out rapid fire instructions for each move as we went through it. She reminded us that we are pulling our lower body down and our upper body up away from each other. We are breathing relaxed. We are zipping up our lower belly like we are zipping up a tight pair of jeans. We are flattening our body like an oval, not round like a tootsie roll.

Whew! It was work! After class I told George, we are going to be sore tomorrow!

I drove us to a branch of our bank.

Normally I used the neat photo option for deposits. But selling a house might have exceeded the dollar limit on the photo deposit. This check required we visit the bank.

It is interesting now. People/clerks seem to recognize I am the one in charge... that something isn't right about George. I am the one they address now. It used to be that even if I talked and did the transaction they were likely to address their questions and comments to George. I hated that!

Now they seem to sense that I am the one making the decisions.

At Jason's Deli I learned that a buffet line is kind of like a bookstore or library for George... too many choices. When I got back to the table I saw he only had a little bit of lettuce, olives, and egg on his plate. I went back to the buffet with my plate and got more of some of the stuff he likes to give him.

Afterward we went up and got the free ice cream. A behavior that George has taken on since his dementia is that when he gets food at the counter, he stands there and starts eating at the counter. When I filled his ice cream cup and handed it to him he stood there and started eating it...

"George, take it to the table," I instruct. He starts walking and eating.

I ask George if he needs anything while we are out. He said he needs shorts. I know he doesn't need shorts. We already bought him shorts on this trip. I do know he needs underwear and socks.

We go to a shopping mall nearby

We walked into Dillard's and found a pack of three pair of underwear in the style that George wears. We had to hunt for a counter with a clerk where we could pay for them.

I pulled out a twenty dollar bill. And I thought the clerk said "Twenty Seven." which I thought was a lot for three pair of underwear. But I pulled out more money and handed it to him.

He said, "I said FORTY SEVEN."

"OH!"

I was in shock and pulled out two more twenties and handed it to him.

Our underwear in a bag we walked out the store...

My purchase I suppose supported them keeping this much inventory....

I told George, "Boy those must be pretty sexy underwear to cost that much!.. maybe they are magic!"

We walked around the mall. There was a store dedicated just to shaving....

We went into a sporting goods store looking for socks for George. At least now I was thinking to look at price tags....

I am beating myself up about not looking at the price tag on the underwear. Not walking away when I heard the price of the underwear....

We left the mall and thought we would try to find a cheaper store to find socks. On our way back to the car I saw a sign for Walmart. Years ago when Walmart came to Wisconsin, I boycotted them. The cheap prices were on the backs of laborers working 35 cents a day and such.

NOW I am thinking, their underwear doesn't cost $50!

We go inside. We get nuts and a package of Dove dark chocolates. I get five mum plants to replace flowers that are aging out in our hosts' garden. We get George some socks, we get a shirt for me and pair of shorts for George (he still thinks he doesn't have enough shorts).

Then we look at the underwear. Six pair for $14.

"Let's get these and take the other ones back to Dillard's," I say.
George agrees.
So it costs about $74 for five bags.

I take a picture of the $50 underwear before we return them...

When we return them, the clerk asks why. I say, "We aren't the kind of people that spend that amount of money on underwear. They must be designer underwear, and we don't have a designer budget."

I felt kind of bad. I would LIKE to be a person who has so much money that designer underwear would be my thing. We TRIED real hard during our working life to become those people. We said the affirmations, we saved, we took the classes, we made the investments and we worked the extra hours.

As it is we are much more fortunate than much of the world and probably three-quarters of the United States. It is silly, stupid, ungrateful and obnoxious to be anything but grateful and pleased with where we are in life.

The clerk told us that they have a Dillard brand of underwear that is much less expensive. I did not tell him that we already got our replacement underwear at Walmart.

He gave me a ticket. He was not allowed to give out cash.

We went up the escalator to customer service and GOT OUR MONEY BACK!

Back at home I had work to do. I had to do bookkeeping regarding the sale of the property we sold in Wisconsin.

George's daughter called and chatted with me and then George. George had been reading his book when Jodie called. I could hear her end of the conversation as well as his. At one point I heard George say, "Take your feet off the couch" or something like that. He had been looking at his book while she was talking and had started to read out loud.

Tomorrow we have breakfast with our Wisconsin friends, Sandy and Steve, who now live in Arvada, Colorado. I will set the alarm on my phone. We don't want to be late for this very important date!

Day 89 - Breakfast with Friends

The alarm on the phone woke us up. Oh yes, today we go to Louisville to meet up with friends, Sandy and Steve. We have lots of memories of laughter and good times. I was excited to see them.

Sandy had selected the meeting place to be in the old downtown of Louisville at Huckleberry Cafe.

We arrived in plenty of time. We walked around a bit. The old town is restored and obviously a destination place with lots of restaurants and a few shops.

As we were walking back toward the restaurant, we saw Sandy and Steve come around the corner. Looking the same with a few more white hairs, just like us...only I have a few more wrinkles too.

During breakfast I thought the window across from me was a mirror or picture. It really surprised me when a little boy came and looked out at us through the window.

The conversation just FLOWED. Isn't that great when you see someone you haven't for a long time and the conversation just runs along like old times?

Steve grabbed the check! Thank you for breakfast, Steve and Sandy!

I mentioned that we might bike in Arvada tomorrow, and Steve showed us where to get on the trail. The trail connects with others and takes us all the way to downtown Denver.

At home George read his book....

I worked on plans for after we leave this place. Using the Affordable Travel Club and Evergreen saves money but takes a little more planning. You have to go to the map and find out if there are any hosts in the area you want to visit. Then you contact them (I usually email an introduction and request to stay on certain dates).

Then I usually don't know what the answer is or if we even have a place to stay for those nights until I hear back from them. Sometimes I don't hear back from them.

As I plan the trip gets longer. There is so much to see.

I get some nice supportive emails from friends and family. I find out a childhood friend is following our journey.

Today I remembered that Saturday is our anniversary. I plan to take George to an old car show. There will be music and we can bike too.

Day 90 - Unsinkable Bus and Denver Ride

I told George we were going to drive to Arvada and bike to Denver from there. After breakfast, without prompting from me, he went out to put the trikes in the car. One of his front tires had a flat, and he changed that without any supervision from me. I cleaned up the kitchen and gathered up our stuff.

Just before we left, I thought, I better check the weather. It said 90 percent chance of rain with winds gusts of around 20 mph!

It is time to create another plan. I did want to see the Margaret Brown museum in Denver. I looked up the RTD (Regional Transit District... or Department). Anyway they have a nice "Plan Your Route" button on their web site. I put in where we were starting and the address of the Museum and it told me which bus to catch where and when.

I said good bye to Gus and grabbed all the stuff I had packed for the day.

I put twenty bucks in the machine. It cost $5 for an all-day pass... and some change. The change for my $20 came out all in coin... $1 coins! I had not seen those in a while! I hope I don't mix them up with quarters!

The bus computer in a nice clear female voice announces the next stop. We were supposed to get off at the "Civic Center."

A nice thing about riding the bus I don't have to focus on traffic.

Downtown the bus stopped and several people got off. I looked around and we were the only ones left. I mentioned that to George. Then the bus driver said, "This is the last stop."

I may have looked panic stricken. She asked, "Where are you supposed to get off."

"The Civic Center," I told her.

"That's this stop," she said. We got off in front of this huge building.

In front of it was this majestic looking mall, "Like the mall in Washington, DC, only smaller," I commented to George.

Complete with the homeless using the area to sleep.

Inside the building we went through security. The guard told us this was a courthouse. I told them we were tourists, and we just wanted to look around. He said they don't get many tourists in this building.

One of the guards asked us to remove the water thermoses... there were three cylindrical things in our back pack they wanted to see closer. George poked around in the bag a bit. I don't think he knew what he was doing it for.

I said, "George they want to see our water bottles."

George poked around a bit more. He then stopped searching. He hadn't a clue. The guard looked at me. She understood; I saw it in her eyes.

I told George to pull out the water bottles, but still he stood like he didn't know what I wanted. I dug in and got the thermoses. The guard said there is one more. I dug deeper and pulled out a can of bug spray.

Oh yeah, we use this back pack to hike in the woods. I should have cleaned it out first.

We could not take the bug spray with us. She told us to come back within half an hour to get it or they would have to confiscate it.

Each floor had huge hallways and marble.

On the fourth floor is a digital readout of all the court cases that were going on and which courtroom... It looked like a lot of tenant/landlord cases.

Back on the street we wound our way to the Margaret Brown Mansion/Museum.

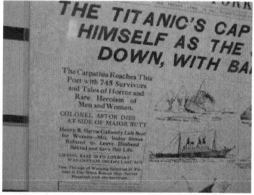

I was not allowed to take any pictures during the tour.

Margaret grew up poor and went to work in a tobacco factory after the 8th grade to help support her family.

Then she went to join her brother in Leadville, CO at the silver mines. There she met Mr. Brown, a mine manager.

She was in her forties and separated or divorced from Mr. Brown when she was visiting Egypt and got news that her grandson was ill. She caught the first ship to the US she could get... the Titanic.

Her life boat had 27 people put on it before they launched it. It had the capacity for 65. Since the ship hands and passengers were not trained about what to do in the case of an emergency, they didn't fill the life boats to capacity.

Margaret was one of the only well-to-do passengers that became active in a movement to advocate for drills and enough lifeboat space on all ships.

The tour guide showed us an embroidery hoop that was 18 inches around. That was the goal of Victorian women of that time to get their waist cinched to 18 inches; TINY! It ended up scarring and damaging the insides of the women. I have no idea how they ate at dinner parties with their intestines cinched shut. The fainting couches were for when the corset was removed. With the sudden release women often fainted.

It was gorgeous out! We could have biked! Where is that rain and cold???

I tried to figure out where to pick up a bus to ride home. I gave up and said, let's walk to Union Station. It was almost two miles away.

We arrived at Union Station. I spent about 15 minutes searching and asking around for the right bus.

I walked around in circles, asked several people and finally figured it out.

The lot where we had parked was the first stop!

We got off and we went hunting for a bathroom. No, this busy bus stop with a parking garage has no facilities.

We got the trikes out from the van. We were going for a ride.

It was a "stop, look at the map, turn around and go back because we missed our turn" kind of ride.

I cheered when we got to the trail; I thought all the wrong turns would be over. But the Ralston Creek Trail has lots of turn-offs, zig-zags at street intersections, and they aren't well marked all the time.

We went through a park with a disc golf course that was very busy. A guy said, "You aren't on the bike trail. It's back there."

The trail where we live has no branches. Which I suppose can be boring for some. But it is easy... you just ride ride ride and then you turn around and come back. There is no map reading, no missed turns...

It was getting more urban looking. Sometimes when we went through an underpass, I felt a little scared. In the dim light I could see sleeping bags, trash and sometimes a shopping cart.

All of sudden we were on Dry Creek Trail..... Not in the plan... I study the map and we can do a loop back to the car instead of an out and back. That's cool!

And then, BAM, without warning, a road block.

I tried going beyond the road block until I could see that everything was REALLY torn up.

On the way back I took a zig zag route to avoid high-traffic streets.

The sky is starting to look pretty gray, and we can see rain in the distance. Crossing busy streets was dangerous. We were crossing with no light traffic light. I would yell to George..."Going half-way." I would go to the middle "suicide lane" where you can turn either way. There I would wait for the traffic on the next half of the road to clear.

George would follow me... and sit with his back end out in the traffic lane behind us. I urged him to move up next to me, and at the same time worry he would move too far forward into the traffic in front of us.

We survived.

Then the wind started up and in two minutes the temperature had dropped at least ten degrees. It started to sprinkle. I asked George if he wanted to stop and put on his jacket.

"No, I don't mind getting a little wet." he said.

We were not far from the car, but after a while I stop and tell George I am getting cold and I am going to put on my jacket. He says, "Me too."

We make it to the car before it really comes down hard. We are cold.

There is evidence that George over-soaked his incontinence pad. I had asked him if he needed to use the bathroom every time we passed a facility. "No," he always said even when he had to wait while I used it. I point out the spot and then say nothing else. It is what it is.

I put a towel down in on the passenger seat.

At home I make pasta and sauce. George takes a shower without any prompting from me. He comes downstairs in blue jeans. He looks clean and neat and good.

Later we drink hot tea, and he tells me he feels better now.

Tomorrow is our 40th wedding anniversary. I tell George we don't need to do anything special because we have been celebrating for 90 days.

Day 91 – Our 40ᵗʰ Anniversary

It's Saturday, August 20, 2016. George said "Happy Anniversary" first thing this morning.

The brain cells affecting his sexual drive have not died.

Gus the cat likes to drink from the faucet. So he talks to me until I turn a little stream on for him. Then I want to pet him, but he swats at me. No petting while he is by the sink!

I made smoothies for breakfast:
- spinach
- tofu
- vanilla yogurt
- celery
- frozen cherries
- 1/3 banana
- 1/2 tangerine
- chocolate chips

I liked it. George made a bit of a face, but ate it without complaint.

I drank coffee and read the paper while George read his book.

We got a Skype call from our Wisconsin friends Mark and Jane! Jane didn't yet show me pictures of her new granddaughter, but promised to send me some in an email. She reads this journal so now she has a reminder.

It was nice seeing them and chatting with them. Skype is so Star Trek to us folks who used to write letters with pen and paper and share a phone line with our neighbors.

Mark asked George if we had always wanted to move to Florida. George may have started out answering the question... but in the effort to talk he lost what he was saying and ended up telling Mark we live by a nice 46 mile paved trail. Mark has visited us and knows about the trail.

After lunch we packed up our bag of stuff off we went to the Rec Center. As we were going in, a couple was coming out with twin blonde girls about two or three years old with bright pink ribbons in their hair and bright pink polka-dot sun glasses.

"Those kids are so cute," George said. We both smiled.

We lifted weights, and then I drove us to Longmont for a Social Club meetup and old car show.

Notice in this picture the watered landscape on the left and the natural Colorado on the right.

The car show was hosted and held at Oscar Blues Brewing. In some places it smelled so strong of the ... what is it? Yeast?

I learned about this event because the Longmont Social Meetup group was meeting here. I looked at the web site to see if they indicated how we would find them. There was no note about a flag or a bright shirt, nothing.

George looked at the back of this vet and knew it was a new one. We both laughed at the license plate...

Then we saw a Tesla fully electric vehicle. Some guy that was looking at it with us said he saw it being tested and it was amazing. "They are powerful cars," he said, "I'd love to have one if I could afford one." A sign in the trunk had a map showing the locations of charging stations.

We went inside to hear the band and look to see if we could recognize any of the Longmont Social Club folks we had met before.

We didn't see any. I sent a message on the Meetup site saying I was there with a hat with flowers on it. "Please come up and say hello." I wrote.

We hung out a few more minutes, walked through the bar one more time.

Then I said, "Heck with it! Let's go biking."

It was a really nice trail. It was smooth, shady, and had interesting things to look at.

At seven miles we hit a dead end...

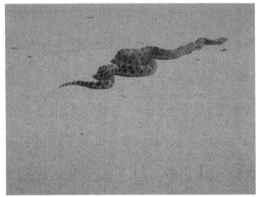

It is turn-around time.

We try a different branch of the trail that takes us through a commercial area. I told George, let's get ice cream....

There were no ice cream shops. We got back on the trail and...

We went back a bit and tried a different branch...

Nope...

We rode the trail back toward the old car show where our van was parked.

I remembered seeing a neat neighborhood on our drive into town. I saw it just before we arrived at the car show. I went looking for it...

And found it...

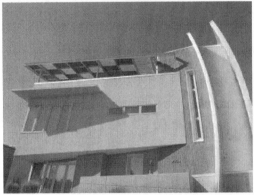

We went by a park and I recognized it as the park we went to and listened to music with the Longmont Social Meetup Group. They have music on the park every Thursday. How cool is that!

We found a house that was narrow and deep with the big front porch in front and the garage facing the back. It was for sale. I pulled out the brochure and I asked George to guess the price...

$350,000 was his guess.

If that kind of home is in your price range, I highly recommend this neighborhood. It looked friendly and inviting. People were out chatting with each other. This particular model had a flat over the garage that the owner could rent out.

We biked back to the car -- 18 miles.

In downtown Longmont we stopped in the used book store. At one point, George left my side and did his slooooow walk up to the clerk. I thought he was going to ask them if they had a restroom. But he was going to ask about a book or type of book. Only when he got up there, he couldn't remember what it was he was going to ask. He stood there smiling and looking at the clerk unable to formulate his words.

I picked up a couple more books from this neat "Little Free Library."
One of the books is <u>The Poisonwood Bible</u>

I told George, "Here are our choices:
- We can wait around and attend the musical playing in Longmont tonight in an hour and a half.
- We can go back to Broomfield to that neat Mini Putt and play Mini golf.
- We can see what is playing at the movies and go to movie
- Or we can just go home and read."

George said nothing.

We got in the car. I went through the list again. George just looked around. It wasn't lying down in his brain... or he had tuned me out? Were there too many choices?

I put my hand on his shoulder. I said, "So???" He laughed a nervous little laugh.

"Do you have a preference?" I asked.

"No," he said.

I drove home. As I pulled into the driveway George says, "Want to go to a movie?"

I won't kid you. My emotion was anger, though I tried not to show it. I explained to him that that was a choice that I gave him before we left Longmont. "Now we are home, we are staying home," I said.

And that is what we did. I uploaded pictures, George read.

Tomorrow is our last day of activity here at this location. On Monday I will be cleaning and packing.

I am feeling a bit sad about leaving here. Beyond here, our trip will most likely be short stays of one to three nights. There will be lots of packing and repacking. There will also be some awesome sights and experiences.

Tomorrow I want to ride if the weather will cooperate. Then... maybe I will take George to another movie.

Day 92 – How Many Turn Arounds Is Too Many?

Gus came in the bedroom mewing this morning. Then he went into the shower and rattled his water bowl. "I guess it is time to get up," I said.

At least he waits until 6:30 or 7:00 a.m. to get us up.

While I was making coffee and smoothies for breakfast, George paced.

At breakfast George told me he was out of handkerchiefs. Use tissues, I told him.

While he was eating, I put a load in the washer in the basement.

While eating my smoothie, I tried to come up with a plan of action for packing and cleaning in the next couple days. I wanted to leave first thing Tuesday morning so we could do a scenic drive in the mountains.

For today, I had heard the Cherry Creek trail was really nice. It is a long way to get there, but we have all day. We had ridden part of the Cherry Creek Trail when we had biked in Downtown Denver. It seemed like a straight-forward easy to follow trail.

On the way to the trail we saw a train hauling a lot of windmill arms.

We were getting close when the road I was on didn't end at Dam Road like the iPad showed. Pretty soon I was going to be on an interstate or in a park and ride.

I chose the park and ride.

I had to use the bathroom, but these park and rides do not have facilities. We rode toward the park first so we could use the bathrooms there.

It wasn't far to the park, but the park is big... very VERY big with lots of trails and roads....

Searching in the park, I finally saw some bathrooms in a campground. But the trail we were on did a big circle around the campground. After quite a bit of riding and worrying, I found the way into the campground. Whew!

When I came out of the bathroom, George said his side didn't have paper. I hurried to my bike and pulled out the paper I carry with me, thinking that he must need it. He started to go into the baggie that holds the paper. I said, "Take the whole bag in with you."

I was trying to rush him. I didn't want an accident to clean up after.

George went in the bathroom and then in a flash he was back out again.

"Wow, that was fast!" I said. "Did you go?"

"No." he said.

"Why'd you need the paper?" I asked.

"To blow my nose," he said.

We rode around the park looking for the Cherry Creek Trail, only I couldn't find it. There were lots of trails and roads. I stopped at a ranger station.

I asked for a map of the Cherry Creek Trail and directions to it.

She said it is trail number six on the map and we are at the East Entrance.

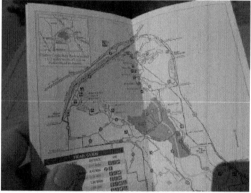

I studied the map... I could not figure out how to get to the purple trail.

I thought I had it figured out. I thought we might even be on it and then...

... a dead end.

We started off in several false directions, then turning around, studying the map, and becoming frustrated. I thought I was on the right trail that would get us there...Dang!

We headed back toward the car because I remembered seeing a sign that pointed toward the trail when we were on our way into the park.

YES! We found the trail! It only took us eight miles of riding.

We started to go down a long gradual hill toward Denver.

As I was speeding down the hill I saw a branch. Two bikers were standing at the intersection.

"Which way is the Cherry Creek Trail," I ask. They pointed to the turn off. I quick make the turn and kept going down.... and then up and up.

I came to another branch. I pulled out my iPad, but I couldn't find us. Some bikers came by.

"Which way is the Cherry Creek Trail?" I ask.

"Depends on where you are headed," one woman said.

"We want the Cherry Creek Trail to Denver," I said.

She pointed back the way we had just come...

"I don't understand....We just were told that this was the Cherry Creek Trail."

And the woman told us there are a thousand branches to the trail. Not all the intersections are marked and you may see that you are on the Cherry Creek Trail, but it isn't the trail to Denver or your destination.

ARG!

"We have over ten miles in and we haven't found our way on the trail yet," I whined.

George said, "Let's just go home."

We headed back toward the car. I pulled up next to George.

I told George I was so tired of dead-ends and turn-arounds. "I just want a good ride."

George said it again, "Let's go home."

"You mean home to Florida?" I asked.

He said, "Yes."

I said, "What about the train ride? You still want to do the train ride through the canyon, right?"

George said, "No."

Then I started laughing and tears came to my eyes and I stopped the trike and gave him a hug and kiss. "YES! Let's go home!"

My mind was a whirl. Were we really going to quit and head home?

By the time we had packed up our bikes it was past lunch time. I hunted for a Jason's Deli. There was one about four miles away.

I parked the car near Jason's Deli and started walking to the door when I heard one of my feet was making a metal scraping noise on the cement....

I guess I was a little pre-occupied when I was putting my street shoes on. I had on one sandal and one bike shoe.

After lunch, I found the address of a movie theater, 10655 Westminster. I could remember the street, but I couldn't remember the number. George is the number guy. So I told him the number and asked him to help me remember it. He repeated the number to me.

We walked out of the restaurant and I said to him, "Are you sure." Meaning, are you sure about quitting this vacation.

"Yes, 10655," he said.

I laughed.

Once I got the GPS programmed I turned to George with my hand on his shoulder.

"Are you sure you want to go home to Florida after we leave Broomfield?" I asked.

"Yes." he said.

"You don't want to bike Zion Canyon?"

He shook his head.

"See the Black Canyon?"

"No," he said.

"Ok then! We made it to our 40th anniversary and now it is time to go home!"

We both smiled.

Back at our home base, I got busy notifying hosts and motels we have a change in plans and will be heading east, not west.

Tomorrow we clean and start to pack and prepare for our journey home.

Day 93 - Cleaning, Packing, and Singing

It is the last day of our house sit. We didn't clean much while we were here, today is the day to clean and to start packing up our stuff, which is spread all over the house.

I pulled out the vacuum and George came and put his hand on it.

"I am going to do that," I said. He let go and went and sat down and read.

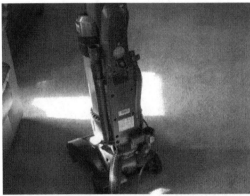

This is a big house. There are lots of floors to vacuum. The footstool where Gus likes to lay needs extra attention....

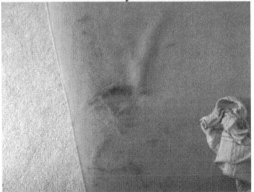

In between cleaning and packing, I had a few things I needed to print out and do some banking before we leave this private Wi-Fi source.

I had written a letter to Kirkland Pest Control -- the company that was charging me to spray for roaches but was obviously not entering the place and the place is now infested... When I got them to go in to take care of the infestation, they actually handed over another invoice!

We will see...

I assigned George to create a couple more postcards.

I got a call from my son Jeremy and his daughter Abby! It was good to hear their voices. They are both getting ready to start school for the fall.

When George was showing symptoms of dementia but before we had a diagnosis, he had taken about $40,000 of our retirement savings and put it in a fund under his name only. Today I tried to change it to my name or to a joint account. The POA paperwork does not allow for putting stuff in my name as the POA.

George took the aluminum chairs we had bought here and started to put them in the car.

I told him, "No, wait until we get the bigger stuff in there. Those go on top."

He put the chairs down on the grass next to the car. Since it would be several hours before we were packing, I picked the chairs up and put them back in the garage.

- Laundry
- Make the bed
- Pack the clothes
- Clean the bathrooms
- Wash the floors
- Clean the kitty litter
- Take out the recycling
- Take out the compost

I had George dust.... I figured if it didn't get done well, that was OK. Be very careful of all those knick-knacks. He dusted for two minutes and said he was done. So I asked if he had done this and that and he said "No."

- Make lunch and eat lunch
- Clean the kitchen
- Pack our kitchen stuff and food

George cleaned the kitchen sinks.

George took out the kitchen trash.

We got new shorts for George last week, and they were too tight in the waist. I moved the button an inch.

I looked at the map and plotted our route tomorrow. I want to take some mountain roads on our way to Canon City.

Our kitchen stuff was all packed. I had George carry it out to the car. Then he went and got the aluminum chairs to put in the car...

"NO!" I said a little too forcefully. "Not yet, and I tried to explain my logic... we have to put other stuff in first... bigger, heavy stuff..."

I packed up our suitcases except for the clothes we will wear tomorrow and had him take them out.

I went out the door to help him load up one of them, and I had just been about to clean the bathroom mirror, so I had a rag and the Windex I set on the front porch.

He picked it up to take to the car to do the windows in the car. But the car was sitting in the hot sun and if he did it now it would be a streaking mess.

I said, "NO George!" And he looked at me angry and hurt. Oh my...

I explain why he shouldn't do it now and that I had it out because I was going to do something with it.

He comes into the bathroom with me and watches me work.

Finally the house is looking neat and clean. Our stuff is gathered in only a few places. I have brought our air mattresses in to spend our last night on them, so we don't have to wash sheets in the morning.

At 4:30 I mapped our route for errands, dinner and a movie.

We went for Mexican again -- Tres Margaritas.

I only had one. The waiter tried to talk me into two... It is happy hour and the second one is only $1. But I am driving... "solo una por favor."

$32 with tip.

Even with one margarita I was feeling too numb to drive. I decided we would walk the two blocks to the Post Office to mail the postcards.

We get back to the car and I heel-to-toe a straight line in the parking lot. I guess I am ready to drive.

Right next door is a filling station. I go in to pay, George pumps the gas. Today he said, "They have to pump it."

"You can't get it to go?" I ask.

"No, they have to pump it," he said again.

I looked and he hadn't lifted the lever on the pump. Once I did it the gas started to pump.

Then I drive to a movie theater.

The seats are amazing. Huge, roomy, comfy recliners with electric buttons that lean them back and raise the feet. There must have been only 30 to 50 seats in the theater... maybe less.

The movie was based on a true story of a woman who was wealthy and thought she could sing beautifully, but was awful. It was funny.

After the movie I do a little opera singing and we both laugh.

Gus is at the door to greet us and rubs against our legs.

Prescriptions For Alzheimer's Disease

You may be wondering if George is on any of the medications currently used for Alzheimer's patients.

I won't go into the kinds of medications and what they do. You can easily research this on the internet. I will say that George was prescribed both Aricept and Namenda when he was first diagnosed with the illness. These are the only medication types available for dementia at this time. They don't cure the illness, they may (or may not) slow down the progression of the illness.

George took the first bottle of each and then when it was time to refill he didn't refill. I asked him about it. Already his communication wasn't what it used to be and he could not express his why, just that he did not want them anymore.

George has always been one to not take medication. I can probably count on one hand how many times he took a pain killer during our 40+ years together. His mother was always taking medications, and George had felt that the medication was causing much of her problems. So when he decided early on to not take the medication, I knew this behavior and belief was in line with who he was and not a symptom of the dementia.

George has been lucky to be healthy for most of our time together. He currently only has the glaucoma medication. I had to push him to consistently take that when it was first prescribed. Missing doses of that could leave him blind, so in my mind he does not have the option of missing doses.

Day 94 – 95 Nature's Beauty

I woke around 7:00 and looked at George. He opened his eyes. I said, "Today... we are OUT OF HERE!!"

He smiled and laughed and we hugged. "I love you," he said.

Packing went smoothly enough. George filled the water bottles and said he was taking stuff out to the car.

I only had to move a few things around after he put them in the car. And at 8:00 a.m. we yelled goodbye to Gus the cat and we backed out the driveway.

We were happy, we were moving again! Two blocks down the street, George said, "What about the garage door opener?" It had been clipped to our visor and we never used it.

At least we didn't get far! "Good job, George!" I said.
Turn around number one for the day...

After I dropped off the opener and yelled goodbye to an elusive Gus, we went to a Village Inn for breakfast.

If toast always lands butter-side down, and cats always land on their feet, what happens if you strap toast on the back of a cat and drop it?

—Steven Wright

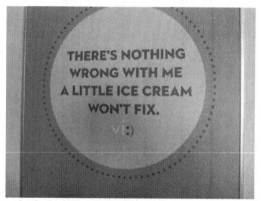

THERE'S NOTHING WRONG WITH ME A LITTLE ICE CREAM WON'T FIX.

Now we were fueled, full of coffee, and ready for the drive into the mountains.

I was also ready to deal with a few turn arounds… three wrong turns before we got out of town. Then it was straight on.

Instead of taking the interstate I wanted one last look at the mountains. I had mapped our route to take a few scenic byways on our way to Canon City, which is just southwest of Denver.

I don't know why rocks and trees and sky and water make us swoon with their beauty. But I was snapping a lot of pictures from the driver's seat, Oooo-ing and saying, "Oh my, so beautiful."

Center City was interesting. The city has filled the small canyon and is now digging into the cliff-side.

I saw some stairs. A chance to move around.

At the top of the stairs was a residential street. I know how much landscape walls cost. This was not a cheap place to build. I was thinking they must mine gold here.

We got into the car to find another place to park. As I weaved the streets looking for parking we were amazed... flabbergasted... totally surprised.... Casino after casino after casino!

We turned down the old main street. MORE casinos! We have been putting loose change in a baggie. I said to George, we should pull out that bag and play a few slots for fun.

"No," he said.

We were taking Central City Parkway toward Interstate 70 that would take us to a back-road pass over a mountain.

It was obvious they had spent ALOT of money to create the Central City Parkway. I suppose it was to get the buses from Denver to the casinos.

This was one mountain road that did not go along a river... the river didn't cut the right of way, man did.

Just before we got to Interstate 70 there was a sign advertising a casino that said it was a Colorado State Casino...

Oh... the State of Colorado owns casinos????

In Georgetown I almost kissed a goat at the visitor's center. I picked up a map of how to get to the scenic byway.

569

It was 67 degrees. We dug out our sweatshirts.

Back in the car we went through old downtown Georgetown to get to the scenic mountain pass.

A couple of switchbacks later and we reached a nice overlook of the city.

As we walked back to the car, George was yawning a lot. I told him to breathe deep. We stopped and did a few of the breathing exercises that Greg Brown had taught us. I have been neglecting the exercises.

What a beautiful experience. I was so glad we took this slower, winding route!

George was having fun, too.

There are two parking lots at the summit. The lower one had about seven vehicles in it. One was an ambulance. One was a sheriff's car.

We saw a helicopter zig-zagging along the cliffs in front of us. A guy with a huge backpack was standing watching.

We drove on up to the upper parking lot. There were kiosks and a pit toilet and about only four other cars in this lot. I kept saying to George how even though this is closer to Denver than Rocky Mountain National Park, there are a LOT less cars and people.

We got out of the car it was SOOOO quiet. Like the moments after a freshly fallen snow.

No big trailers or RVs are allowed on this route. No trucks.

George kept saying, "We are above the tree line."

The kiosk said that a plant the size of a quarter could be thirty years old. The season is so short, the weather so challenging for life. PLEASE STAY ON THE PATH!

573

We went on a quarter-mile path. When we got back the parking lot was empty except for our car and a truck with a "Mountain Rescue" logo on the door. He got out and said we would probably want to move our car because the helicopter was going to land and sand blast everything.

I asked if they found the hiker.

He said, "Yes." And he said, "You have a whistle? ....Lifesaving... a $1.50 whistle and a garbage bag," he told us.

We started going down the other side. The byway ends in Grand, Colorado.

I was looking forward to some hot chocolate or something sweet to drink. I was feeling a bit of nausea from the altitude change.

Grand had nothing. The next town was ... I think Jackson. It is a blink-and-you-miss-it ranching town.

I pulled into a gas station...

No hot chocolate. No chocolate milk...

I reverted to the remedy for altitude sickness that my mother taught me. I know, my friends in Florida who think we eat healthy will be shocked. But yes.....

It worked. We burped, I felt much better.... and a little guilty too.

We were still at 9,000 feet, but were on a long plateau with ranches of horses and buffalo and cattle.

We checked into our motel in Canon City.

I told George we were here for two nights. It was misty and the tourist office was closed.

I was sorry I had reserved two nights. I told George I would try to change it to one... but I was tired, and so I delayed the decision.

We went for a walk to explore.

The park across from the motel was setting up to have a band play. We could hear the music from our room.

"Tommy Tight-Wad says... quarters are the cheapest way to call long distance."

My plans to eat something light for supper went out the window. We had those Cheetos at around 3:00 p.m.

It was raining. Everything seemed closed in town. So we walked to the closest open restaurant and we ordered pizza.

OH MY! A 16-inch was like 30 inches in diameter. They must have used a whole pound of cheese.

We boxed half the pizza and with no way to save it, we walked down to the park where we had seen two homeless guys... or travelers.

Because it was raining they were gone from their spot. We walked around looking for them, but didn't find them. On the way back we saw two teenage boys hanging out under the bridge and I asked them if they wanted it.

"Yes! Thank you!" they said.

I don't think they were homeless, just teenage boys... always hungry... especially for pizza.

Back at the motel I checked my phone. The manager of the one remaining homes we have in Alabama called. The offer that he had gotten in spring is still on and the buyers want to close on the 31st.

I am to call the closing agent tomorrow.

Because it was raining, we went to our room. I uploaded pictures to this blog, 115 pictures! That goes to show that the views were so wonderful today. We had fun.

Day 95, I am so tired while writing this that I don't think I can remember much of anything about this day.

I was able to cancel our second night at the motel; the clerk refunded half our money.

Canon City had a three-mile long river trail. We needed to exercise. After checking out I drove us over to it and I told George it would be a vigorous walk. We did a good pace and pumped our arms.

We came across the start of a fitness track. Yeah! We did some of the exercises.

There was a sign by the pit toilet. I thought that was strange and I went over and skimmed the sign... something about number 2 and pushing a red button.

I went into the toilet and looked for the red button. I went back out and read the sign more carefully....

OK, this has to be a joke. "It's inside the rim of the toilet???" I said to George and laughed...

But still, I went back in, practically sticking my head in the toilet to see if there was a red button under the rim...

We both had a good laugh. I am so gullible! A woman came by, and I told her about the sign. Whoops, she was on the phone with those earphones. She stopped her conversation to listen.

Then I heard her tell the person on the phone that there was this nice couple on the trail doing the exercises....

On the walk back we slowed our pace and I make some phone calls.

I called a long-time friend, Bev, and we chatted most of our walk back to the car.

I had gotten a call from the manager of our property in Alabama. So I called him back.

I called the closing agent and gave her my email.

Then we went to the Canon City Library. I had stuff to print, sign, scan and send. This closing agent doesn't have the internet techno-savvy like another agent I have worked with. Signing online when you are traveling is easier than using libraries.

But this was pleasant and George went to the magazine section and spent the time browsing magazines.

After I emailed the signed and scanned papers I had to step outside and call to make sure they got the documents. I also called Bill, one of our travel club hosts that has been following our blog and had some questions. He recommended I go through with the divorce.

It was almost noon by the time I went back inside the library to get George.

It wasn't long and we were out of the mountains.

We passed some muddy crowded yards of cattle. Awwww, I said. So sad.

We stopped in La Junta and took a walk and visited a museum.

It cost $3 each to go through the Koshare Indian Museum.

It turns out that the museum is actually about an Eagle Scout program in the area. Buck Burshears taught boys in Boy Scouts about Native American Arts and Culture and then started the museum.

Each Boy Scout had to create something in the same way as the Native Americans did. In this way they learn how much work and time went into this craft and learned to appreciate the art much more.

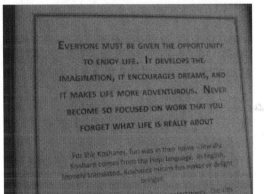

After our break, we got back in the car. I asked George, "continue east or head a bit south and hit Texas?" George said he had never been to Texas.

I set the navigator for Amarillo, Texas.

After just two turn-arounds, we were going the right direction...

We went through several "National Grasslands."

We stopped at a wayside to eat our supper of PB&J with spinach and banana on top.

There were signs at this wayside that explained how it came to be that the government owns so much of the grasslands in the area.

It was in the 1930's when the farmers in the area were turning the soil just like they would have done to farm back East. Only in this area... when a drought occurred, that soil began to blow away. The big dust storms of the time turned the sky black miles away.

The farmers were devastated by the drought. A man lobbying in DC about the issue was giving a speech when the sky turned black from the dust being blown all that way.

Congress agreed to buy the land from the farmers and work to heal the land. The farmers were able to move elsewhere and start new lives with the money they got.

Now the government rents the land back to ranchers for their cattle.

We went through one town with streets so wide you could get THREE combines to fit side-by-side.

We saw antelope.

I started to sing a few lines, "Home, home on the range... where the deer and the antelope play..." George laughed, but he didn't join in this time.

The air started to smell like a huge slaughterhouse, for a long way. Then it smelled like natural gas... and then something else... kind of chemical.... Yuk!

Night and we are still moving...

I had set the navigator for one motel. When we arrived, I didn't like the neighborhood. There were bars on the windows on the shops nearby.

We found another motel by the airport. $112 per night.

Ahhh, no thanks.

Next motel, a Day's Inn seemed just as nice but was only $65 for the night plus tax.

It was 10:00 p.m. when we checked in. We were going to stay two nights because we had driven so much today.

Amarillo was flat, treeless, and something smelled. We just got one night.

I was SOOOO tired but wired from all the driving.

Our room is nice and roomy and neat.

Later I noticed, the tub wasn't just dripping, but dribbling. I didn't want to deal with it. We turned the fan on in the bathroom and closed the bathroom door to shut out the noise. I will tell them about it in the morning.

Day 96 – 101 - Drivin' drivin' ... drivin'

It is Thursday, August 25, 2016. I decided to head toward Oklahoma City. I saw that Oklahoma City seemed to have some bike and walking paths. That's a good sign that we would find things to do there.

After a day of being in the car I cheered when we passed a sign saying we were entering Oklahoma City.

The motel is clean and roomy and $65 a night. I paid for two nights.

It looks like there is stuff to do here. Maybe we will stay three nights, so we don't have to worry about finding a place on our way on a Saturday night.

I say to George, "Look at us! Here we are in the United States."

Smiles.

Stuff to see here and a trail to ride nearby!

Day 97 - Sand Spurs in Oooooklahoma City

Last night after our walk we had discovered sand spurs all over our shoes. These are very sharp, very hard, burrs. They cut right through our tires and puncture our tubes. I should have remembered better and stayed on the pavement.

The trail goes through a neighborhood of post WWII homes.

I watched this dog laying on someone's roof for a while to make sure it was breathing. I guess it's a nice quiet place to keep an eye on things... when he isn't napping.

I noticed George was far behind. I waited for him. He was going pretty slowly. He was eating an apple I had given him.

As he pulled up I said, "Did you release your brakes?"

He said yes he did.

I pointed to the brake on the right side. "Release your brake," I said and pointed.

"I did," he said. I kept pointing; he released the break.

Then I noticed the left front tire was very flat. "You have a flat tire," I told him.

"I know," he said.

"Why didn't you stop and change it?" I asked.

"I did," he said. Then he started pedaling.

"George, you need to change that tire," I said.

"I know," he said.

I had to pull up next to him and make him stop.

We put the bike in the grass and as he changed the tube, I checked our tires for sand spurs.

There were lots of pieces of sand spurs stuck in the tires. I picked at them with my thumbnail to edge them out enough to grab them.

We pedaled to downtown.
We kept pedaling, right by a baseball stadium.

I took lots of pictures for my friends, Dick and Bruce, who follow the games and are big Cubs fans.

We found a bistro for lunch.

When we got back to the bikes, three tires were low. We took turns pumping the air into them.

I wanted to check out the memorial for the Oklahoma Bombing that occurred in 1995.

I took the picture below just as George was losing his balance. Fortunately he did not fall. A behavior that is part of George's dementia is that when he climbs stairs he does not put much of his foot on the step, and with each step he puts less and less of his foot on the step. I coach him, but it makes no difference. I should walk behind him, so he doesn't fall backward down the stairs. I guess instead he would fall on me.

I was reminded that one hundred sixty-eight people died in that bombing.

After the memorial I started taking us toward the Cowboy and Western Living Museum. But we had to stop twice to pump up tires. It was time to head back to our motel.

Even if we would have stayed on the pavement, there are areas where the grass grows through cracks. There are areas where someone had mowed and the path was littered with clippings that might contain lots of sand spurs.

Even with the tire challenge we are having a great time riding. It feels good, the sun isn't too harsh, and there is a lot to see.

We arrived back at the motel around 3:00 p.m. My tires needed pumping again. We put the bikes in the car to rest until we get back to Florida.

We got a call from our Florida friends, Debra and Glen. After chatting with Debra I turned the phone over to George to talk with Glen. I heard George say several times, "We sure do miss you, I'll tell you that."

I went out to the front desk and changed our reservation again, we head out tomorrow.

Day 98 we headed out at the sun was rising. As we were leaving town on Interstate 40 there was a "Silver Alert" on the digital sign overhead. Silver Alerts go out when an elder person goes missing, usually due to dementia. My thought was that in a few years that could be my George they are searching for, or my friend's husband. I also thought that as the baby-boomers age silver alerts will be much more common.

I had mapped out a route to take us to a scenic byway through some mountains (or hills) just south of the Ozark National Forest.

To get to the scenic byway we were going to be taking the Indian Nation Turnpike.

What I thought, as I drove the turnpike was, "This doesn't seem like the way Natives would want to treat the land..." A lot of land on either side of this wide highway was cleared.

We got off the Toll Road.

The scenic byway starts in Talihina.

In Talihina we parked the car and started to walk around to check out the small town. We were in the Choctaw Nation Area.

We found an interesting coffee shop...

A guy was walking away from the shop and told us it was closed. He was just going there for a cup of coffee and was disappointed.

He asked where we were from, and we chatted a bit and said we were looking to get breakfast somewhere.

He said he would walk with us and show us around. He introduced himself as Brian. He is of Choctaw ancestry. He showed us Pam's cafe. We went in Pam's cafe and he asked if he could sit with us. "Sure!" I said. (I would like conversation for a change!)

He was bubbling with information. He's a chef, he likes to clean, and he's a recovering alcoholic. The casinos have helped build the community hospital and built the recovery clinic where he goes to get help fighting his addiction.

He told us Talihina means steel road ... there used to be an active railroad that ran through town.

I asked Brian about the toll road, "was it Native Americans that pushed for it or the US government that pushed it on the tribes."

Brian said the Government decided the road was going in without the approval or desire of the tribes.

He listed all the different tribes and said they have a chief. He confirmed that this was the end point on the re-location of tribes to Oklahoma. He said the Choctaw were removed from the Mississippi area.

We enjoyed all his conversation and bought his breakfast.

Then we left and he left with us, and he wanted to know where we were going next. I told him we would walk around a bit more. He showed us this and that and mentioned a museum.

"Oh! I'd like to go to the museum!"

He was the self-appointed tour guide and took us over to the museum.

He walked around and picked up brochures and gave them to me. I tried to resist. I didn't want all that paper. If I wanted to learn that stuff, I can look it up on the internet, I thought.

But after trying to refuse once, I didn't know how I could continue to insist without seeming rude and interrupting his dialog.

The museum was closing. I felt a need to end our time with Brian. We walked around a couple blocks but I felt we had to cut our walk short because I was starting to feel uncomfortable that this stranger would not shake loose.

The Talimena Scenic Drive has LOTS of scenic overlooks.

The area was green and humid. Below is a picture of a large brown rubbery mushroom.

The scenic byway crosses an old military road. The military road was created by soldiers who were paid an extra 1/2 cup of whiskey and 15 cents a day for the hard work.

A kiosk stated, imagine looking out and everywhere you see there are no trees, only stumps. That is the way it looked when the lumber barons were done with the land...

Then again, the Government came to the rescue. They bought the land and planted the trees... The US Forest Service was born.

We pulled into a wayside and looked down this walk and there was the back end of a black bear trotting away from us.

So cute (he/she must have been young)! Our sighting was so brief. The bear quickly disappeared over the hill.

The scenic byway crosses into Arkansas.

We stopped and took a trail down to a pioneer cemetery. People had left stones and coins on the markers. I don't know if this is a Choctaw tradition or a southern tradition.

Further down the road we came upon an old car show!

George was walking pretty wobbly. I am thinking it is because he was so busy looking he was thrown off balance a bit.

I took the picture below for my friend Debra, who likes teal.

Every time we passed this car, George said he used to have one like that (when he was a teenager).

The third time, I got the hint. "You want your picture taken with the car?"

"Yes," he said.

We arrived in Mena which is at the East end of the Scenic Byway. We got a motel room. It was expensive, $99/night with 10% discount for us old folks.

We sat out by the pool in the shade and ate our Subway sandwiches. Then I went for a swim.

I was uploading pictures for this blog when George said, "What are we going to do this evening?"

"You want to do something?" I asked.

I drove us closer to downtown, and we got out to walk.

And what do you know... we came across a band getting ready to play!

The car show we saw was part of an all weekend event that included music and more show time in downtown Mena.

We enjoyed watching people. Pink hair, 50's hair, balloon people...

I said to George, "These people have a lot different lifestyle than the folks in Steamboat Springs, Colorado."

He laughed and agreed.

601

The music was country and a mix. Moms were dancing with their little kids.

We passed a woman with a low-cut gown and breasts that were obviously enhanced. I caught myself trying to look without staring, but it was hard because one breast looked a lot larger than the other.

After we passed I said to George, "I was trying to figure out if they were the same size..." I wondered as I said it if he had noticed because sometimes he doesn't see things...

He smiled his boyish smile and he said he was trying to figure out the same thing.

Interesting... seeing where his toothbrush is or where his medication is even when it is right in front of him, is difficult... but put a pretty woman in a crowd....

By **Day 99**, I must be looking pretty lonely. When we stopped at McDonalds for breakfast, Earl, who retired from a career in the Air Force almost 49 years ago, came over to chat with us. He said to look up <u>Black Bird Rising</u> to get a picture of the plane he worked on. He is 86 years old.

We drove over rolling hills and through small towns with populations less than 500 people.

We listened to another book by Sue Grafton... <u>F is for Fugitive</u>.

We stopped at a Denny's for lunch. The air vent was sweating, and the salt was so damp it didn't move in the shaker despite having some rice kernels mixed in.

The landscape got very flat and the road was always above the surrounding fields and forests. "We are getting close to the bayou," I told George.

We landed in Lafayette, and we were so tired of sitting. I stopped at a shopping center, and we walked around before looking for a motel.

The ditches showed signs that they had been full of water recently. I looked on the map and the flood disaster of 2016 is already in Wikipedia and shows this area was part of the declared flood disaster area.

I wondered if the motels would be full of construction and relief workers.

The first motel we stopped at was full. The second had a room for less than $75 with tax.

I tried to haul up everything we would need in one trip. My hands were full with iPad, waters, camera.... And I had to gather up this stuff too. It took a few drops and frustration, but I did it.

As we walked in all loaded with stuff, I saw the luggage carts by the motel door. Dang what a doofus I can be!

We have laundry to do and some closing paperwork to attend to.

I found "Myth Busters" on TV and that kept George happy for over an hour.

I have noticed a new development.

When we go to bed, I hug and kiss George goodnight. Then I settle down to read or play solitaire on my iPad. I had stopped reading and doing electronics in bed as part of the insomnia study I had participated in. But now that we have been traveling, I find it helps. Since George needs more sleep than me, we go to bed at the same time.

Only now he watches me read until I kiss and hug him again and say goodnight a second time.

I just wonder, as his short term memory fades are we going to go through a nightly ritual of ten kisses and hugs??? Not that this is a BAAAAD thing.

Day 100 I had to take time for business. I was awaiting the paperwork from the closing agent for the sale of our last bit of rental property. Hurray!

We went to do laundry and on the way back to the motel we passed a Planet Fitness. I saw a sign that said they are offering free workouts to seniors over 60 during the month of August.

When I went in the clerk said it would be $20 each. I asked about the sign.

The clerk said, "Oh yeah, I forgot about that. You get in free."

After about 25 minutes George walked slowly up to me while I was doing leg lifts and just stood watching.

"What do you want?" I asked.

"I'm done," he said.

I told him to go sit in the lobby I had more to do. I worked out 25 more minutes. He was just sitting... waiting, with his hands folded.

While I was stretching, I had thought about going to get him because I KNOW he didn't do any stretching.

But I selfishly just did the stretches on my own.

Back to the car I checked my email. I had an email with the closing documents attached. I went back to the motel to print them; two guys were standing over the motel computer looking at pictures of pretty women... four pictures to a row and rows and rows of them.

"Are you on a dating site," I asked?

One of the guys said, "Naw, those are friends of mine."

The desk clerk asked if she could help me, I told her I was waiting for the computer. I needed to print something out.

The guys got off the computer.

After looking over the documents we drove around to several banks before we finally found a notary; she charged $20.

Last rental property sold!

I was relieved..

George had a craving for sweets; I got him some cookies, and I picked out a treat for me...

I liked the name. I didn't realize until I got back to our room that is said 36 proof! Oh my!

I mixed it with lots of water and I am sipping it as I do this post.... Can you tell????

On our way back to the motel from the grocery store, I tell George I don't like Lafayette. He says, "I don't like it here either."

I said, "They don't have many sidewalks; the streets are not in good shape, the houses aren't in good shape; there are no bike lanes or bike paths. Drivers are in a hurry and honk at me..."

Every few minutes he says, "I don't like it here."

We get in the room, and George heads for the cookies. We had already eaten one in the car.

"No, wait a minute and I will fix you something," I said.

George just smiled and hovered while I put together a salad and had him heat the leftover pizza slices.

I made him sit at the desk to eat and reminded him to lean over his plate.

These are new interactions for us. Call me the bossy lady.

I stand at the TV stand to eat. It is too quiet. I turn on the TV to see the weather.

George gets up and stands in front of the TV with his salad. I have to guide him again to put the salad down and lean over it as he eats.

I got an email from Bobby and Glenda. They were our very first Evergreen Club hosts on this trip! On day one we stayed with them. They have been following our trip. They offered to host us on our return trip in the upper peninsula of Florida. How kind is that?!.

I got an email from my friend Debra saying that there is a tropical depression that will be sending major rain to western and upper Florida. It is supposed to hit Wednesday... if it hits.

I google how far we have yet to go to get home, over 600 miles. That is too much to drive comfortably in one day for us.

We have driven over 10,000 miles on this trip. Today is day 100. I see some comments on Facebook from friends thanking me for taking us with them on this trip. I would have gone bonkers if I could not have brought you with us.

It is **Day 101**, Tuesday, August 30, 2016 and we are 600 miles from home.

I checked George's incontinence pad while he was in the shower and threw it away. It is full almost every morning now. I have to check it and change it or guide him through changing it.

We packed up and use the motel cart to take one trip to our car. I am ashamed of how bulky I have packed. Two days in one place and I brought in the cooler and the snacks and the dishes, besides our suitcases and water bottles and electronics.

I will need to retrain myself if we or I ever tour on our bicycles again.

On Interstate 10 we headed east east east into the sun and bayou country.

We crossed a long bridge over the wet land.

I pulled in at a welcome center that was not open yet. There was a sign outside that said that bridge we were just on is the third longest in the US. We were on the first longest on the fourth day of this trip.

There is a road to a boat ramp between the eastbound and westbound lanes of the Interstate 10 bridge.

I turned off the interstate and found a low-traffic road.
We passed sugarcane fields and then we stopped in a visitor's center.
We went to a lock museum.

A guy named Stanley greeted us and took us around the museum and showed us the lock and levee.

The end of the lock, by the Mississippi River, now dead-ends at the new levee. It was built after the flood in 1975.

We went further down the road and stopped at Nottingham Plantation.

The owner was from Virginia. He strategically married to get a $20,000 dowry and lots of slaves.

I learned that southern plantation owners were required to pay a tax after the Civil War. His tax was $20,000 and a personal visit to DC to apologize.

I learned that after the war, Cuba's slave traders and slave owners came and offered to buy up slaves. A southern slave holder could sell his slaves or set them free. The owner of Nottingham offered a choice to his slaves to continue to work for a wage or leave. Most stayed and worked.

In Donaldson we stopped at the Grapevine Cafe.

Most of the tables were working men meeting over lunch. Stanley had told us the area was first rich in lumber, then oil and now there are lots of chemical companies in the area including Dow.

The menu had no vegetarian options. The waitress was good, without a blink she offered pasta with grilled veggies. Yes, we will have that.

Leaving Donaldson we passed some of those chemical plants. One was making gases of some kind. We drove about one-quarter mile with highways of pipes traveling above us like a pipeline interchange.

SMACK! We both jumped. A construction truck way in front of us was tossing rocks and one of them got our windshield.

George, without prompting from me, picked up the camera and took a picture.

We went for miles and miles along the beach. AND THERE WERE NO PEOPLE!!! No swimmers which is understandable because there are warnings of undertow because of the tropical storm out in the Gulf. But there were no runners, no walkers, only a handful of sunbathers.

IT WAS WEIRD!!!

At 4:30 I had enough driving for one day. Best Western had a senior rate of $64.

The tropical storm is expected on Thursday afternoon.

I told George tonight, I am tired of sitting in a car all day! Even though we get out and walk and see things, it is just a LOT of sitting.

Then I come in and sit and blog.... just call me crazy.

Day 102 - Click your heels, George!

Wednesday, August 31, 2016, we made it home! Yes! We made it home without major incident and all in one piece.

Though, I think by the time we arrived, we were both about to scream from sitting in the van so much.

I didn't know we were going to make it all the way from the border of Alabama. I was planning on just driving until I got tired.

I had George pop in a book on CD to listen to. It wasn't a mystery or anything that grabbed us, but we listened and it helped pass the miles and miles.

When we crossed the border into Florida I let out a "Woo-hoo!" It's a long drive down the panhandle of Florida.

The Florida love-bugs were all over the front of our car.

When we got on Hwy 19 it started to rain.

The landscape was lush and green. They had gotten a lot of rain in Florida this summer.

When it is raining out it is harder to get out and walk around. We were both adjusting our seats and squirming.

I said to George, "Click your heels, George! And say, 'There is no place like home.'"

He laughed and said, 'No place like home, ya."

We celebrated the landmarks on our way: turning off Hwy 19, going through Dunnellon, passing the pink elephant on Highway 41.

It was almost 5:00 by the time we pulled into Inverness.

Home! The grass is long and wet. The bushes are scraggly and need trimming.

The pineapple I planted five years ago finally gave us a pineapple.... only we weren't here to harvest it. It lay rotting on the ground, taking root.

The collard green plant in the backyard is long and leggy.

My trike had two flat tires; George's trike had one.

If you have never unpacked with someone with dementia let me just say, it is an experience.

I was rushing in and out. George stood over the mail opening it.

I paused and told him to be sure to keep all the mail in that spot; I have to deal with it later, I tell him.

It used to be that George was very methodical about unpacking. He'd empty his suitcase completely before moving on to anything else.

Now it is different. He would go to a bag of groceries and pull things out one at a time just looking carefully at each item and set it on the counter. Sometimes he would just pick something up off the counter and look at it a while and set it back down.

He had removed his suitcase but didn't think to unpack it. Then when I started to unpack mine, he came in and unpacked a few things and then got distracted.

He tried to unload the trikes before we had cleared an area around them and removed the stuff on top of them.

I would see him walking around in a daze holding something and ask him where he was going with it and direct him to the right location. I was worried that stuff would get lost, and I would spend all my time looking for it later.

I needed to chill and not sweat the small stuff.

George sat down to read. I think he was aware that he was foggy, and so he sat and read his book. Maybe I had said, "NO!" too many times.

I started to look through the mail. Oh my, I had been ignoring the list I had made that outlined when I send a check, where and how much. I had the list with me and used it the first month.

But then the planning and the traveling and the doing took over... and besides that, in my own defense, we had closed on the sale of two houses while we were traveling and and and....

So, opening the mail I found that one of our bank accounts had been closed because I had started the process of getting POA over our joint account. I guess I didn't fill the paperwork out perfect. So Fidelity decided they didn't want to continue with that account. This, of course, is the account with all our automatic bill payments set up. So we had bills that were not getting paid. That is going to be a headache to correct.

Then I found bills for George's gap insurance. They had looked like junk mail, and so they were not forwarded to me but were put in the junk mail pile. I don't blame the people sorting our mail. I should have called them when I noticed I wasn't getting a lot of mail from Blue Cross.

The insurance company was canceling George's insurance as of.... 8/31/16.... TODAY!

It was already evening. The offices and banks are closed. I kept telling myself to chill, it will all work out. Don't worry....

Sometime we must have gotten a call from George's daughter, Jodie, who left a message. I called her back. I left her a voicemail and told her we made it home safe and that the storm surge that was coming to the west coast of Florida was going to hit land north of us.

I am sure as I left the message I sounded frantic. Trying to unpack, keep an eye on stuff George unpacks, and worrying about the bookkeeping mistakes I made.

Maybe I couldn't relax because I had pushed myself to stay alert the last hour or two. Statistically most accidents occur close to home. On a long trip it is easy to start thinking ahead to what you will do when you arrive and not pay as much attention to the road.

Later, lying in bed, I kept mentally going over how I SHOULD have done better. Then another part of my brain is telling me things like:

"What's done is done."
"It will all work out OK"
"It is no big deal."
"Belly breaths"

I got up and read until after 1:00 a.m.
Tomorrow I will try to straighten out this mess.

The Journey Continues

This has been quite a journey. We have gotten to visit with family and friends, make new friends. We have seen incredible sights from bayous that went on for miles and miles to mountain vistas.

During our trip, George has lost more of his brain cells, and I have had to take on some caregiving tasks. Bit by bit I am taking on the role of caregiver.

I have had time to adjust to the diagnosis and to new symptoms. Through this blog I have been able to share not only our geographic trip but our journey through the cognitive losses and adjustments.

Our future is unknown. I know that this Alzheimer's and aging journey will continue.

One thing that prompted this trip was our pact to get divorced if this kind of thing ever happened to one of us.

As you may recall, I had said that after George's definitive diagnosis I brought up the idea of divorcing him for my financial security....George had tearfully requested that I wait until after our 40th wedding anniversary. That anniversary has come and gone on this trip.

Divorce is still an option, but I don't think I can do it. Even as he is leaving me, my love for him is growing. How can that be?

George has always been so proud that we have stayed married and in love through the good and bad times. I don't think I can or want to take that from him. Though a legal divorce may be the most logical to protect the assets for my future. Emotions sometimes (most the time?) rule over logic.

I still have decisions to make... do I work to create a better financial future for my old age by getting a job now? Or do I stay closer to home and take care of George and enjoy him while some of him is still with me?

Do I keep my fingers crossed and hope that my health and strength will remain good, so I can work when he is no longer under my care? Old ladies check out groceries, work reception desks, run for President even.

And you may be wondering... Do I continue to record our journey for our family and friends and the world to see? Yes, yes I do.

It has been helpful and enjoyable to share this journey with you. From your comments, I know it has been helpful, eye-opening, and even enjoyable to you.

I don't want this connection to you and this journal to end. So I will continue to write about our experiences on occasion. Please join me as I keep <u>Alzheimer's Trippin' with George - The Journey Continues</u>.

Before you set this book down and walk away, please leave a short review on Amazon. All it takes is one or two sentences. Don't give the story away...Thank you, Susan

Acknowledgements

Thanks to the family and friends that took this journey with us. You know who you are! You called, you emailed, you read and commented on the blog, you made us a meal, put up with us in your home, gave us hugs, and spent time with us.

Thanks to Mary McNeece and Margaret Juhl for their support and doing the tedious job of editing these many pages. How did we get so lucky to have been graced with such giving friends!?!

Thanks to the members of the Evergreen Club and the Affordable Travel Club that hosted these really strange strangers and extended an open heart, compassion, direction and friendship.

Thank YOU for reading this book and allowing me to express my joys, fears, frustrations and heartaches without judgement. You are awesome!

About the Author

Susan Straley started to journal at age 16. In 2016 she journaled online as a platform to bring her family and friends with her and her husband, George, on their road trip across the U.S. Susan Straley lives, enjoys friends, writes and bikes in Inverness, Florida.

She has written a sequence to this book to be released in June, 2019.

The Journey Continues
Alzheimer's Trippin'
With George

Dementia Caregiving With Friend, Family and Community Support.

The Journey Continues after their 10,000-mile road trip, Susan and George strive to live fully while navigating new dementia symptoms. Susan openly shares the moments of joy, worry, gratitude, and frustrations.

As she winds her way over the challenging moments does the caregiving burden become overwhelming? Does she come to depend on Depends? Will their friends and community step forward to support them? If so, how?

And the biggest mystery of all, will you and George and Sue find that life still has great joy in the midst of weariness, uncertainty, and change?

Reviews of
Alzheimer's Trippin' with George
The Journey Continues

"I was telling my husband about your books and your and George's story...even the part about showering and how he would only wash what he could see. How many people realize or even think that? Or the importance of the stretching exercises to maintain balance. Or you honesty and love about your sexual relationship. " Karen Kline R.N., B.S.N. Faith Community Nurse, First United Methodist Church, Homosassa, Florida. Coordinator Memory Lane Respite and Support Group

"Let me start by thanking you for sharing your special story of love with me. You certainly captured many details in lessons in what true love is. Your relationship with George was clearly unique and precious and your honesty about the last few years of your relationship and how love carried on was inspiring." Kathryn Quinlan staff member at Positive Approach to Care

"Susan's journey encompasses the stress and love of being a caregiver to a loved one. My favorite line is her eating cookies and reading tips on weight loss when your life is upside down you look at the world differently. Eat the cookies!" Theressa Foster CEO of West Central Solutions an Assisted Living Facility management, consulting and oversight firm.

Before you set this book down and walk away, please leave a short review on Amazon. All it takes is one or two sentences. Thanks for being part of this trip. **Susan**

625

Made in the USA
Columbia, SC
17 February 2019